Praise for *Ma*

"Whether your marriage is highly conflictual, loving, or painfully distant, Sherry Cassedy gives you medicine for the heart. Her personal and professional experience makes her a wise healer. Your renewal begins the moment you start reading this exquisite book."

—Ellyn Bader, PhD, co-founder of The Couples Institute

"What a relief! My wife and I are not alone! Sherry Cassedy lifts the veil of secrecy about the universal experiences that go on beneath the surface of a marriage. Her hard-won wisdom will resonate with all marriages, including our long-term same-sex marriage."

—Marge Slabach, commissioner (ret.)
of the San Francisco Superior Court

"Sherry's honest story about her own marriage entertains, intrigues, and deeply touches the reader, inviting us all to examine our own situations. A brave and tender book."

—Helene Brun, MS, life coach
and former couples' counselor

"Every engaged couple needs this book. Sherry's insights on marriage from her personal and professional experience will resonate with everyone who says 'I do.'"

—Jim Moroney, publisher emeritus,
The Dallas Morning News

"Sherry has extracted wisdom from her years of experience as a leading marriage advocate and offers the fruit of her dedication as a distinctive gift to the world."

—Eileen Donahoe, former ambassador to the Human Rights Council, and John Donahoe, CEO, Nike

"*Marriage Unveiled* takes you alongside Sherry and Matt's marriage, their challenges, and their choices, plus shows the tools they used to grow into a more connected and intimate relationship."

—Kyle Benson, couples therapist, writer and producer of relationship blog *Intentionally Intimate Relationships.*

"A unique, intimate, and brave look at marriage. The author's insights from her long-term marriage and career as a family lawyer make this book authentic and very readable."

—Joan B. Kelly, PhD, author of *Surviving the Breakup*

"Insights flow from every page in Sherry's unique and powerful voice, at once pragmatic, feminist, and deeply spiritual. Whether you are embarking on a new marriage journey or already riding its sometimes rocky waters, *Marriage Unveiled* offers a fresh perspective that feeds the soul."

—Geniveve Joan Ruskus, JD, family lawyer, former president of AAML Northern California

"Sherry Cassedy courageously uses her own marriage to show how, over time, couples may go from the heights of romance to the depths of grief and still maintain hope, companionship, and love."

—Drs. Gloria and Heidi Horsley, co-founders of Open to Hope

MARRIAGE UNVEILED

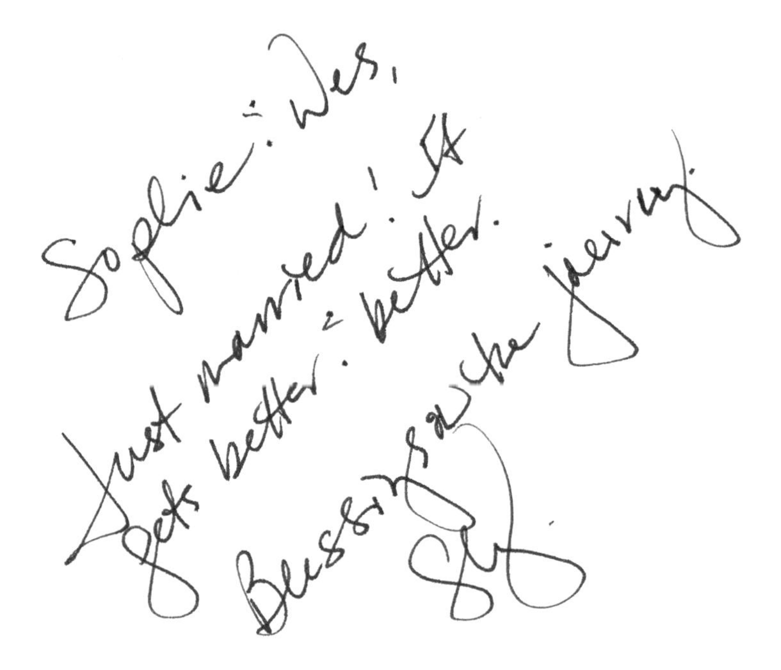

MARRIAGE UNVEILED

The Promise, Passion, *and* Pitfalls *of* Imperfectly Ever After

Sherry Cassedy

Published by River Grove Books
Austin, TX
www.rivergrovebooks.com

Grateful acknowledgment is made to the following sources for permission to reproduce copyrighted material:

Excerpt from "Poetry and Marriage" from *Standing by Words: Essays* by Wendell Berry. Copyright © 1983 by Wendell Berry. Reprinted by permission of The Permissions Company, LLC on behalf of Counterpoint Press, counterpointpress.com.
Excerpt from "Returning" by Jennifer Berezan. Copyright © 2001 by Jennifer Berezan. Reprinted by permission of Jennifer Berezan.
"Wind" by Judith H. Lasater. Copyright © 2020 by Judith Lasater. Reprinted by permission of Judith Hanson Lasater, Ph.D., PT.
Excerpt from *The Quest for the Mythical Mate* by Ellyn Bader and Peter T. Pearson. Copyright © 1988 by Ellyn Bader and Peter T. Person. Reprinted by permission of Ellyn Bader.
"The Third Body" from *Eating the Honey of Words: New and Selected Poems* by Robert Bly. Copyright © 1999 by Robert Bly. Used by permission of HarperCollins Publishers.

Distributed by River Grove Books

Design and composition by Greenleaf Book Group and Mimi Bark
Cover design by Greenleaf Book Group and Mimi Bark
Cover images used under license from ©Shutterstock.com/creativestockexchange; ©Shutterstock.com/Evgenyrychko

Publisher's Cataloging-in-Publication data is available.

Print ISBN: 978-1-63299-556-8

eBook ISBN: 978-1-63299-557-5

First Edition

CONTENTS

For Matt, my enduring partner in love and life. For our three children, Tyler, Cassedy, and Timothy, who have contributed profoundly to our marriage. I am most grateful to each of them for the love and acceptance they have shown us, and for the singular place they each take up in our hearts.

PREFACE

Matt came up the stairs into our bedroom looking agitated, holding the phone away from his body like a detonation device. I had already dropped into bed, my refuge after a long day, and settled into my nightly read. Normally, Matt would respect my momentary solitude, but that night, he barreled determinedly toward me as he emphatically punched buttons on the phone and handed it to me.

"Listen to this message," he demanded.

Taking the phone from my usually calm husband, I listened. I heard a woman's high-pitched voice with a short but powerful message:

"*Hello, Dr. Sullivan. This is your secret admirer. I've been watching you, and I'm hoping we can get together real soon. Bye.*"

His eyes, always intense, were searching for some explanation. I was also searching his face for a clue of what he was thinking.

"Can you believe that?" he asked, his voice uncharacteristically rising.

"Pretty wild," I responded, caught off guard but trying to sound neutral.

"I've listened to it over and over, and I can't figure out who it is."

There was almost panic in his voice. He rambled on that he was worried someone was trying to set him up. Maybe a disgruntled client was tempting him into a trap, to shame him and bring him down. Working with high-conflict parents, he was always on guard for personal or professional attacks. He said he didn't recognize the voice.

I tried awkwardly to reassure him, telling him not to jump to conclusions and just wait to see what, if anything, happened next.

He calmed down and got ready for bed.

I was also a little flustered. I wondered what this might bring, whether knowing that someone saw him as cute and sexy might change him in some way. That's why I'd left him that silly message. Over our 20-year marriage, Matt had maintained his trim swimmer's body and a youthful spring in his step. He was serious about his work. With piercing blue eyes that seemed to see right through you, he brought that same intensity to everything he did, from cooking for the family every night to his morning exercise regimen and his commitment to his clients. He was a good man, a good husband. I realized how much I loved him and how little I showed it. He deserved to be cherished and ravished, and so did I.

Twenty years into our marriage, we had settled into certain roles and routines that were comfortable and predictable. But under the surface, I was struggling with a rising restlessness that Matt found threatening to our well-established lifestyle. We had dealt with threats to our marriage before: early conflict and later drifting apart, both of which created vulnerability to infidelity, more as a symptom of our lack of connection than a threat in itself. Each time, we had managed to stay true, recover, and recommit. That distance was growing between us again. I was hoping to rekindle the passion in our marriage as we struggled with this midlife passage. Started on total impulse, this flirtation was unpredictable, holding both promise and peril.

1

WE MARRY THE UNKNOWN

> Marriage . . . must be an unconditional giving, for in joining ourselves to one another, we join ourselves to the unknown. We can join one another only by joining the unknown. What you alone think it ought to be, it is not going to be. Where you alone . . . want it to go, it is not going to go. It is going where the two of you—and marriage, time, life, history and the world—will take it. You do not know the road; you have committed your life to a way.
>
> **—Wendell Berry, from "Poetry and Marriage"**

This quote is the consumer protection disclaimer, the warning label for marriage. I often use it when I officiate at weddings, and it should be printed in large type across every marriage license.

Your marriage is not going to be what you think. It is going to be so much more if you are willing to let go of your limited notions. And it is going to be sorely disappointing if you don't.

Americans love marriage, by which we really mean weddings. Americans marry more—and divorce more—than any other culture. We love the romance, the proposal, the engagement, and the wedding day extravaganza: rings and flowers, cake and champagne, poetry and music and dance. We then send the couple off into the sunset with a promise of happily ever after. There, the fairy tale story ends. And, of course, the real story begins.

An actual marriage is a mystery. The alchemy of any single relationship is unique: how we meet; how we know; how we decide, commit, and consummate; how what each of us brings to the altar complements or conflicts with what the other brings; how we create our home, our family, and our mutual journey from this singular combination.

This all takes place behind a veil of privacy. Once married, we don't talk about marriage, and the couple is left to navigate on their own. The veil of silence isolates the couple from essential wisdom and support at times when it is most needed. Keeping the reality of marriage—our joys and struggles—obscured allows the idealization to flourish, with disillusionment and cynicism following close behind.

I always opened the first day of my theology of marriage course with this story: In the beginning, God created Adam. Adam was in the Garden of Eden, enjoying all the beauty and bounty surrounding him, the amazing variety of plants and animals. But Adam was lonely.

He talked to God about his feelings, and God said, "Well, Adam, how would you like to have a wife?"

"What's a wife?" Adam asked.

"Oh, a wife is wonderful! She will be your companion day and night. She will collect food and make delicious meals for you. She will caress your body and soothe your mind. She will love you and be with you always, for the rest of your life."

"Wow, that sounds amazing," said Adam. "How much does something like that cost?"

"Well," God replied, "That would cost you an arm and a leg."

"Hmm," said Adam, "What can I get for a rib?"

We laugh. The story sets us up for the fall. The idealization of marriage is followed all too quickly by a deep cynicism about the meager reality of a long-term partnership. Marriage is veiled in mystique and critique, with little cultural understanding of the realities of married life, the tremendous work involved in creating a healthy marriage, the boundless joy of life's shared blessings and trials, and the strength of having a partner to navigate the journey with. Even as American culture idealizes—perhaps even idolizes—marriage, we do little to support the reality. The unhelpful "happily ever after" mythology is perpetuated—even marketed—in our culture, and it sets up disillusionment and confusion when marital difficulties arise. It can undermine the success of real-life marriage. Even as family and community supports for marriage have fallen away, the reality of divorce, infidelity, family violence, financial stress, and a culture of cynicism have eroded our faith in marriage as an essential social institution.

The word *marriage* itself can be a flashpoint. To be clear, I am referring to the core relationship between two loving adults who make a commitment, whether recognized in law or not, in the presence of their chosen community to spend the rest of their lives together. The controversy over legalizing same-sex marriage may have actually given the institution of marriage a much-needed boost. Younger couples were delaying or choosing not to marry at all, not seeing the value in giving their commitment a legal imprimatur. As gay and lesbian couples advocated to be allowed this legal status, both conservative and liberal proponents defended the importance of marriage, from their divergent perspectives, as the foundation of family and a critical social institution. In the campaign for the right to marry, same-sex couples highlighted the importance of not mere domestic partnerships but of full recognition of their loving commitment. They also sought to demonstrate the legitimacy of their families, as well as to obtain the benefits conferred by the state and private employers to married couples. Across our different circumstances and perspectives, genders, and sexual orientations, we share a common desire for a loving, committed, and intimate partnership.

Marriage is a crucial human endeavor and remains our primary unit of social development. It deserves our support at both the institutional and individual levels. The commitment to marriage provides an essential foundation for family life, a frame for the flow of relationship from the logistics of daily life to the deepest dreams and desires of each partner. The marriage binds and holds the couple in all its messiness and grace within the larger movement of their lives.

I am not a wide-eyed idealist. I have been married for over 40 years, raised three children, and practiced divorce law for 37 years. I know firsthand the joys and the challenges of long-term marriage. I have been intimately involved as an advocate in hundreds of divorces, working to resolve cases by settlement if possible and appearing in court as necessary to decide contested issues. In recent years, I have dedicated my practice to working exclusively as a neutral mediator or private judge, meeting with both parties to the marriage, with or without their attorneys, to resolve the issues and help them move forward in their lives as coparents and as individuals. I have also taught the theology of marriage at the university level, led marriage preparation and support programs, and worked with couples to prepare and officiate at their wedding ceremonies. I have witnessed and worked in marriage from all angles.

Over the same time, my husband, Matt Sullivan, a clinical psychologist, has worked with parents in child custody disputes in a variety of professional roles, helping parents share time and responsibility for their children during and following separation and divorce. We lovingly refer to this as our work in the trenches, in the muddy fields of marital and parental difficulty, inadequacy, growth, and simple successes. I have been honored and humbled to be admitted behind the veil into the intimate chamber of all manner of marriages. I have observed the inner workings, the triumphs and the tragedies of life lived together. I have taken these lessons to heart.

With eyes wide open, I am a fan of marriage. I believe in the ritual and institution of marriage as well as in the process of becoming that a good marriage not only supports but demands. The promise of marriage is that you take each other's hand and begin your journey into the unknown, with trust in one another and faith in the journey itself, to hold you and form you and bring each of you to fullness. Marriage is a process of becoming for both partners as you also support each other's growth. Couples make this commitment to one another and to their future together, taking courage in the ancient teaching that "love bears all things, believes all things, hopes all things, endures all things. Love never fails" (1 Corinthians

13:7–8). This age-old verse might be dismissed as parochial or cliché, but with lived experience of marriage, we come to recognize how profoundly true it is.

Love may never fail, but our limited human capacity for trust, kindness, forgiveness, and perseverance can falter, and without the support of family, community, faith, and understanding, a marriage may fail. No small part of that failure is our failure as a society to better inform and support couples to navigate the inevitable challenges, leaving them to do so with little to no guidance.

In my many years of practice, I have come to a general and sad sense that, of all the divorces I have seen, about half were good marriages at some point and for a length of time. But then life happened, and the couple struggled. They didn't receive the support they needed and, more likely, received well-meaning advice validating their singular perspective and perhaps encouraging them toward separation and a fresh start. Through a cascade of events, they found themselves at a point of no return. The other half of the divorcing couples were never healthy relationships from the start, but pairings arising out of less conscious, even wounded places in the heart that reenacted each person's negative emotional cycles. These marriages were perhaps better ended. While that may have been the healthier decision for these couples, the process was every bit as painful.

As I sit with couples, I do not evaluate or judge any individual decision about divorce. The more experience I have, the more I truly appreciate that only each person living inside their own marriage can make that decision. But occasionally, I get a glimpse of the former love and goodness, the deep care that they shared for one another, the sincere effort each made to honor their promises, and the sense of defeat and guilt in not being able to overcome the problems. Other times, I learn of hurtful patterns played out over years and wonder how they had tolerated living in the marriage for as long as they had.

How can we evaluate our own marriage, especially in times of struggle? Is this a good healthy marriage going through a normal and maybe even necessary trial or change? Or is this a signal that we have made a terrible mistake in choosing each other and are playing out our worst instincts, destroying ourselves and perhaps our children? Where do we look for guidance? Other marriages? Model marriages that look from the outside as though they have the answers may appear quite differently from inside the veil.

The privacy surrounding marriage obscures both healthy partnerships other couples could learn from and dangerously unhealthy marriages where one or both partners are at risk of being traumatized—physically, emotionally, or sexually—without knowing whether this is normal or seriously dysfunctional. Although each marriage is unique, there are some basic norms for a healthy marriage, including the physical safety of both partners and the children; the dignity of each partner free of emotional, sexual, or financial abuse or control; and functional communication. If these basic elements are absent, the marriage is likely destructive to one or both partners.

The veil of silence becomes an obstacle to accessing wisdom, whether talking with family and friends or seeking a counselor or other resources. Once they are married, it is no longer appropriate to inquire how the couple is doing or how the marriage is going. That crosses an invisible boundary of marital privacy.

Before I was married, my girlfriends and I would share every detail of our love lives. Once I was married, that came to an abrupt end. This unspoken rule became apparent when I got together with my three best girlfriends from high school. We had all been married for some time, and one of us was recently divorced. As we talked, the three of us who were still married all asked shamelessly about our divorced friend's love life while we kept our own marriages securely behind the veil.

The cultural traditions for family or faith community to support the marriage have largely eroded, leaving the couple alone in their struggle. Opening conversations about marriage can provide tremendous relief, humor, and the support to carry on, especially if we trust that the others are loving and supportive of our marriage.

Sometimes, the best approach is honestly sharing our own experience. Stories of long-term marriages can be romanticized, skimming over or idealizing the difficult times. Or, they may be recast from the bitter vantage point of divorce in order to justify a decision to separate. This story will be neither. It is an honest account of the sometimes treacherous landscape of conflict, compromise, reconciliation, and renewal that has defined my own marriage. By lifting the veil and sharing the honest, unvarnished story of my own journey with my husband, a navigation of sometimes difficult terrain over many years, I hope to shed light on the underlying processes, complex motivations, and perilous pitfalls that all marriages must confront.

Matt and I joined one another and the unknown 40 years ago, and the journey has unfolded from there. It has not been what either of us thought it would be; it has been what we have created in every moment as we have moved along the river of life. Our journey is unique, as is each marriage. Our story covers a long arc of time, starting before some of you were born. We come from a particular stripe of America, which may be very different from your own. While our story arises from and enfolds our particular circumstances, the experience and wisdom cross lines of race, class, religion, and sexual orientation.

In marriage, we each construct our own framework from our families of origin and relationship experience, our dreams and wounds. We establish the container of rules, roles, and rituals. This is a constant and sometimes contentious negotiation in the early years of the marriage, but eventually, the unwritten rules are understood and integrated into the fabric of the marriage. A good marriage will always require renegotiation of these boundaries to allow growth for both partners. In other words, a good marriage will always have an inherent thread of challenge, a growth edge to navigate, hopefully together but not without struggle. These growth spurts are natural, inevitable, and critical times for the marriage. If the couple can move through them together, the experience becomes a source of strength and deep satisfaction. These are also junctures that show the fractures in the container and can shatter it, allowing each partner to grow beyond it but leaving the marriage in pieces.

One of these challenging junctures is at the heart of this story, in the middle of our lives. As we approached our 21st anniversary and both of our 45th birthdays, our marriage was running dry, worn from years of strain, each of us pushing the edges in our separate ways. Neither life nor marriage is linear in its progression. Earlier experiences in our marriage contributed critical context for the events we would confront in our relationship's 21st year. I will pick up those threads as we go, and we will look behind the veil of our personal circumstances to tap into the common ground of our human struggle. I have provided reflection questions at the end of each chapter to help you engage your own relationship story, questions, and insights, as well as resources that Matt and I have found helpful along the way. You may skip over them, dive in for reflection, or defer them to another time. They are there to support you as needed and to bring some of my reflections into your experience. Life itself, including the mistakes we make along the way, is our best teacher. Perhaps it is more about asking the right questions than having all the answers.

Whatever state of bliss, contentment, disappointment, or despair you are currently facing in your relationship, you will find resonance with our common challenges and blessings. My hope is that you will walk away with fresh insight and renewed inspiration to navigate your own committed relationship—your marriage.

> ***A good marriage will always have an inherent thread of challenge, a growth edge to navigate, hopefully together but not without struggle.***

Reflection

- How do I define marriage? It can be simple, even a few words.
- How do I envision marriage for myself? What am I seeking in the relationship and the journey together?
- Is my partner's vision similar?
- What are my greatest fears about being married?
- What are my highest hopes?

2

THE MUCK

Second anniversary

Jour et Nuit, "Day and Night," was the name of the quaint little French restaurant in Georgetown, the chic corner of Washington, DC, that had become our anniversary spot. We had enjoyed romantic dinners here for our six-month and one-year milestones, and we were returning to celebrate our second anniversary. In these early celebrations, excited for a rare evening out and hungry for a meaningful conversation, Matt and I had intuitively adopted a ritual of a leisurely romantic dinner accompanied by a year-in-review reflection—the highs and lows, events and emotions of the prior year, and where we found ourselves in the flow of life.

By this second anniversary, there were lots of lows. I was dreading this year's review. A melancholy feeling had been my constant companion for months, knocking persistently at the door of my consciousness. I had continued to push it away. On the way to the restaurant that evening, I opened the door for a peek, and in rushed the awareness of how miserable I was in my marriage. I felt unseen, unappreciated, and unloved.

Tears welled in my eyes, and the truth became suddenly clear and inescapable. I was not in love. I was not even angry anymore. Anger takes a level of energy, an investment. No, even worse than angry, I was indifferent. So, this was it—a loveless marriage. I was stuck. Our one-year-old adorable baby boy was now the only glue that held us together. I realized the grim choice: to leave and raise my son alone or remain in this loveless marriage for the rest of my life. It was a sad fate for a vibrant 25-year-old woman.

Even worse, I felt completely isolated. Although I had good friends, I couldn't share this terrible secret with anyone. To say we were struggling out loud would make it too real and would perhaps set in motion a whole series of events. I couldn't even tell Matt how I felt. He would have been devastated, hurt, and then angry at me. Again, things could mushroom, snowball, cascade out of control, setting in motion the whole process leading to divorce. No, I had decided I couldn't tell anyone. It was better to keep up the happily ever after facade and suffer in silence. The silence, however, was far from golden. It was a thin sheet, and increasing alienation was brewing below it.

As we were graciously shown to the table, chairs pulled, napkins fluffed, menus provided—all the rituals of an elegant meal—the annual review loomed ahead, a dark cloud threatening to drench what should have been a lovely romantic escape. But there was no romance and no escape. The review would reveal the truth about this past year of conflict, daily arguments, and stony silence. Before we were married, we used to watch couples at restaurants and suspect that we could tell which couples were married—the ones who weren't talking to each other, eating in silence, staring at their plates. They didn't engage, because they already knew what the other would say, and they didn't want to hear it. Now we had become that couple.

When we decided to get married, we were entirely in love, full of hope and common dreams. We enjoyed all the same things: music and sports, people and studies. We came from similar backgrounds and values, worked well together, and shared common beliefs and aspirations. We spent every possible moment together, blissfully compatible. Just two years later, work and school had pulled us apart as we each developed more polarized perspectives and reacted defensively to the other's development.

As a second-year law student, I had become involved in feminist politics, which fueled my inborn sense of injustice and contributed to my rage at the ubiquitous patriarchal emblems of society. Matt was in the middle of his doctoral program in psychology, learning to rise above and attend to the larger context of interactions, which suited his more introverted tendencies.

Between my feminist anger and Matt's detached superiority, our communication was contentious and reactive. Whatever I said he immediately heard as an angry political and personal attack. Whatever he said I heard as detached amateur psychoanalysis, aloof and full of judgment. We each cast the other as a stereotype and refused to let them be anything else. Instead of listening to each other, we were building our defenses and our case for the next interaction. It was a vicious cycle, a constant daily struggle. We were so threatened by the other's point of view that we solidified it, wrapped the other in it, and refused to let them disrobe. We were each trying on new professional personas and swimming in the new responsibilities of parenthood and marriage. Were we afraid of truly seeing each other—or afraid of being seen?

Sharing a life, a small apartment, and responsibility for our infant son made communication necessary, no matter how much we sometimes wanted to avoid it. Rather than engaging each other directly, we would talk through baby Tyler in a faux soothing singsong tone, hardly disguising the real message. "Mommy doesn't like it when Daddy is watching TV." "Daddy is going to the store and will be back in a little while." "Mommy will change you; Mommy always changes your diapers." Little Tyler bound us together. He was beautiful—robust, smart, active, and funny. He didn't stress us but delighted us, and we loved the experience of the three of us as a family. But the dynamic between the two of us was infuriating. We realized that Tyler would eventually learn to talk and that this method of channeling was not only ridiculous but unsustainable. We couldn't even agree to get help. Matt, of course, suggested therapy, but I was not going to be teamed up on by two shrinks! I cleverly consented to seeing someone, as long as it was a feminist therapist—my own double-team. Of course, he rejected that idea. We were lost, hopeless, and loveless.

There is a place in married life where most marriages spend some time—a place where the flame has grown dim, where the tensions of work, family, and daily life overtake the attention to one another, where small kindnesses and romance are neglected. I refer to it as "the muck," because that is exactly what it feels like: being stuck, mired in negativity, and trapped in endless cycles of argument that never solve anything but go around and around until the nausea sets in. But there is nothing merry about this go-round. Everything the other does is incredibly annoying—eye-roll annoying, take-a-deep-breath annoying, wonder-how-you-ever-got-stuck-with-this-person annoying. And stuck is the essential feeling. We were stuck in patterns, stuck in our interactions, stuck in our emotions, with no way out. The gloopiness of the muck was constantly pulling us back under, impeding any effort to move or change, leaving us feeling helpless and hopeless.

In my yoga studies, there is a Sanskrit term that describes this feeling: *duhkha*. It means "sorrow, pain, distress, suffering, a bad space." The ancient Aryans, who brought the Sanskrit language to India, were a nomadic, livestock-breeding people who traveled in ox-drawn wagons. *Su-* and *dus-* are prefixes indicating "good" and "bad," respectively. *Kha* is the Sanskrit word for "hole," particularly the axle hole of one of those ox carts. *Sukha*, then, literally means "a good axle hole," whereas *duhkha* means "a poor axle hole." You can imagine a broken cart, stuck in the mud—in a bad space. The sound of the word *duhkha* itself captures the feeling, complete with the sigh of exasperation.

In spiritual terms, this malaise is commonly referred to as the "dark night of the soul," a phrase coined by St. John of the Cross. The brilliance and distinction of this idiom is that it is understood as a necessary phase of spiritual development that we will all experience at some time. We all have the potential to move through it with practice and intention to a better, more enlightened place. Our perseverance will be rewarded. The dark journey will incubate something that redeems us and makes the struggle worthwhile. Out of the muck, a lotus will bloom. We can better tolerate pain if we know it is temporary and is birthing something better.

But this is not an understanding we have about marriage, although perhaps we should. Marriage is a journey that, if not expressly spiritual, is certainly psychological, emotional, sexual, and practical. If we can anticipate a dark night in our individual human journey over time, it might be reasonable to expect that when we merge our life with another, we will also encounter dark nights together, struggling not just with our own inner landscape but the growing pains of both partners. But because, in the marriage, we are wrestling with another human rather than the angels, we somehow think that we can win, we can master this, or we can navigate our way out. And if all else fails, we can leave our partner in the mud, scrape the muck from our shoes, and walk away. What I have found after having spent time in both the spiritual dark night and the marriage muck is that my efforts to pull myself out of it are generally futile, if not counterproductive. Like being stuck in quicksand, the more I struggled, the deeper I sank. The muck requires a different approach.

In marriage, we reach an equilibrium where things are working. Then change happens. It can be a good change, such as the birth of a child, a new job, or a windfall of riches, or it can be a bad change, such as a health crisis, the loss of a job, or the death of a loved one. But good or bad, change forces us to reorganize the system. When the old routines don't work anymore, new behaviors are required that, figuratively, upset the apple cart. As things come tumbling down, the efforts to stop it, to save it, and to get back to the old pattern are futile. That familiar routine will no longer work.

Early in our marriage, with a new baby and two professional degrees in the works, we were ill equipped to navigate the huge chasm between our idealized expectations and the stress of our shared life and ever-increasing responsibilities. We had begun with enthusiasm, decorating our simple apartment and enjoying new parenthood together. But our lives gradually shifted as we each tried to expand into our separate studies and new professions while staying anchored to the daily demands of a new family. There was no going back to where we had been, and we were unprepared for the disorientation of these new changes. We struggled, we flailed, we got angry, and we cast blame on each other, all to no avail. We eventually had to come to terms with the reality of our disillusionment and discontent.

Stuck in the muck, we sat down for our second anniversary dinner. We looked at the menus, not at each other. We fell back on the rituals of the meal, ordering a bottle of wine and our dinners. We waited.

Tentatively, gently, we began the year in review, starting with our first anniversary. That had been a happier evening, a rare occasion to leave the baby with friends. We recalled the year, Tyler's many joyous milestones, each of our studies and budding professional identities, new friendships, visits with our parents and extended families. Eventually, the conversation came around to our relationship and the constant conflict. We admitted what we both knew all too well: that we seemed unable to communicate about anything without quickly descending into argument. We were both feeling hurt and somewhat bewildered by the tension between us. As we talked, we acknowledged that routines helped. Attending church on Sunday morning was often a healing event, reminding us of our better intentions and of the Christian values of forgiveness, selflessness, and love. We were part of a community of couples in our graduate student housing, and we were close enough with the other couples to realize that all marriages had their troubles. We just somehow felt that ours wasn't supposed to.

We talked about some of those other marriages and their struggles. One couple was involved in a program called Marriage Encounter through their church. We vaguely understood it as a process of writing letters to each other to share feelings on selected questions. We didn't know much about it, but it seemed safe enough. Searching for something constructive, we agreed on setting aside a time to talk each week, to try this method. I don't remember if we came to that idea during dinner or sometime after, but we began a new routine.

We committed to spending one hour talking together and settled on Sunday after church while we were in our most loving and forgiving frames of mind. We structured the discussion with one of us posing a question each week for us both to respond to with our feelings—not blame, rationalization, or even problem-solving, just feelings. Arriving back in our small apartment after church on Sunday, we would settle Tyler down for a nap, brew some fresh coffee, and take our corners on our secondhand sofa. We dreaded those hours, but we had made a commitment to try it, so we forced ourselves to do it. It was only an hour! Still, we could easily slip into our argumentative pattern, ending with hurt feelings again.

We attempted to make the questions more positive or at least neutral: "What was the most powerful moment of our wedding?" "What is something I appreciate about you today?" Our answers were often strikingly similar. We both shared about the final blessing at our wedding when the priest laid his hands heavily on our heads, the weight of the blessing descending upon us. We tried to stay with our emotions, to identify and describe the feelings as completely as possible. We described where we felt it in our bodies, what color it was, when we'd felt it before. Our intention was not to explain or blame or solve but to share and describe the feeling. Even constructive problem-solving is a way to avoid feelings. Problems are not solved at the same level of consciousness that created them. Focusing on feelings helped us drop into a deeper level of conversation. This was difficult for me. I realized how much I had shut myself off from my feelings in my nose-to-the-grindstone approach to life.

We would then exchange our letters. Letter writing had been an intimate connection for us during times of physical separation. We both seemed to drop our defenses more in writing than in speaking. We each got to have our say without interruption. Just seeing Matt's familiar all-capitals handwriting softened my heart. We each tried to truly consider the emotions the other had shared, to understand how the other felt, without judgment or attempted solutions. We began to understand the importance of sticking with feelings in our responses; otherwise, we could dip immediately into conflict.

Slowly, we began to talk and to listen to each other. It was tempting to revert to old defensive and hurtful patterns, but that usually meant we had abandoned feelings and moved into fixing or blaming. Dropping below that level of engagement, we started to understand each other's feelings, hurts, and fears—past and present—and to sympathize with them.

Eventually, the hour was not so painful. We began to look forward to this precious time to share deeply together. We were learning to build intimacy, to take risks in sharing our feelings, and to hold each other in an embrace of emotional tenderness. Over time, we relaxed the structure of the conversation, and our communication flowed more naturally. At some point, we stopped the formal practice, but it remained in our toolkit to return to in other times of conflict.

Over the next two years, we dealt with other challenges. I will never forget the morning Matt called me, bewildered, his voice breaking as he said, "My father died." I felt an urgent need to be at his side, to comfort and support him in what was to be a difficult time for him and especially for his mother. After I completed law school, I found and lost job opportunities over several months, creating anxiety for me and uncertainty for our family. We were able to navigate these events together, drawing on the strength of our partnership, trusting in our ability to support each other.

I remember our fourth anniversary as we drove off for our annual dinner date. Preparing things for the babysitter while also trying to dress up for the evening was hurried and hassled. But then, sitting in the quiet bubble of the car, I allowed myself to relax into what I hoped would be a romantic evening. I looked over at my husband of four years, an accomplished student and loving father, about to launch his career in psychology. I felt grateful to have him as my partner. As I began my reverie about prior anniversaries, I recalled the tears of two years earlier. *Hey*, I thought, *I really love this guy. I'm in love! We're back!*

We had been getting along well over that past year, but I hadn't made the connection with my earlier resignation to a loveless marriage. I was surprised. Who knew that it was possible to revive love from the indifference and despair I had felt two years earlier? I certainly didn't, and no one had led me to believe such a thing was possible. But there we were, back in love, communicating from the heart, enjoying being our family of three, and planning to add another child soon.

I had unwittingly subscribed to a fairy-tale expectation of living happily ever after, an assumption that is pervasive in our culture. The newlywed couple's expectations are set unreasonably high. The buildup of the wedding day doesn't help. It can be a magical send-off to a mundane reality. When the natural struggles of daily life descend, spouses can be confused, disappointed, and angry. Unprepared, they can take this out on one another in a cycle of blame and anger that eventually erodes the marriage.

This unhelpful mythology contributed to my disillusionment and confusion when difficulties arose. I thought that, if you married the right person, you would live happily ever after. When we struggled, I assumed I had made a terrible mistake and married the wrong person. The only solution was to go back to the beginning and find the right person or remain stuck in a loveless marriage. Many marriage support books focus on finding the perfect mate—finding the love you want. But marriage is not so much about finding the right person as it is about becoming the right person, as well as supporting your partner to become their best person. Like life, a good marriage is necessarily a process of becoming. Marriage is the work of reconciling the dreams and expectations with the lived reality of human relationships. It will include peaks and valleys, struggles and triumphs.

When I struggled early in our marriage and was afraid that I had made a terrible mistake, I learned a secret not part of our cultural mythology. We could recover from conflict and disillusionment; there was a dynamic flow between the darkness and the light.

As with the dark night of the soul, the dark night of marriage requires surrender. The first step is to acknowledge that we are in a bad place—*duhkha*, the wheels have come off. We need to allow it, to sit with it, to realize that the prior rhythm is gone, and to let it go. Once we acknowledge where we are and let go of trying to return to where we were, we can find a stillness in the muck. Envision a wagon having slid downhill into a ravine with a broken axle. There is no way to stop it or push it back up the hill. There is no use spinning your wheels. Sit there in the mud. Let go. Maybe even enjoy a mud bath or the velvet blanket of darkness. The irony is that if we sit in the muck and allow it to seep into our pores, there can be a kind of peace, a release. And in that stillness, the next phase can germinate.

From the stillness, with patience, insight will arise. From this creative impulse can come the thread of a new understanding that we can slowly weave into a lifeline that we can use to climb from the muck. Once again on firm ground, we can build new approaches, roles, and methods that will become the new equilibrium—until the next change. But with each disruption, we become more skilled, more capable of the work. Eventually, we may navigate an episode so deftly and subtly that we might even fail to notice the night has come and gone. But there will be times once again when we are hit hard, knocked to the ground, and brought to our knees. Then we will need to sit in the muck and slowly crawl through the mud, trusting the dawn will come.

Marriage will always be day and night. The nights are long and dark and lonely, but the day will dawn with new light and a fresh perspective. The night will come again and again, but belief in the rising light of day will see us through. We were blessed to learn this lesson early in our marriage.

> ***The dark journey will incubate something that redeems us and makes the struggle worthwhile. Out of the muck, a lotus will bloom. We can better tolerate pain if we know that it is temporary and is birthing something better.***

Reflection

The reflection questions at the end of each chapter could be shared in a dialogue format.

Adding the question, "How does my answer make me feel?" will make almost any question work for the dialogue process. Remember, it's all about feelings.

- When have we experienced dramatic change in our relationship?
- How did I shift in response to the change? How did my partner shift? How did our routine or patterns change?
- What strategies have we developed to communicate about difficult topics?
- Have we experienced a time of feeling stuck in the muck? How did we handle it or move out of it?

Practice

Marriage Encounter teaches a method of structured communication called dialogue.

1. Set aside an hour of quiet, uninterrupted time together.
2. Choose a question; take turns.
3. Each take 10 minutes to write a letter to the other in response to the question. Focus on feelings. Avoid temptation to blame, explain, or solve. Name the feeling. Describe where you feel it in your body, its color, taste, or other sensation, and when you have felt this before. Open and close your letter lovingly.
4. Exchange letters and read your partner's letter. Read it

again and circle the feelings. Notice which are the most powerful feelings.

5. Decide who will go first. The recipient of the letter questions the writer about the feelings that are shared, but only to better understand them—not to judge or dispute. When complete, the other recipient inquires and shares.

6. End at one hour. Set time for the next dialogue. About once a week is recommended.

For more information and suggested dialogue questions, visit https://wwme.org.

3

PATHS DIVERGE

21st year

Knowing the pitfalls doesn't necessarily mean we can avoid them. The prior year, we had been giddy with planning and preparing for a 20th anniversary gala. We invited friends and family to share in the celebration, complete with formal wear, dinner and dancing, and toasts to ours and other long-term marriages. It was important to us as divorce professionals and marriage advocates to celebrate our 20 years together. It was also crucial to do it publicly, with our community, who had supported us through the years.

Somehow, a year later, we were back steeped in the muck. Approaching our 21st anniversary, we found ourselves disengaged and discouraged. Our communication was strained, seemingly always on the edge of argument. I felt a defensive, cutting edge in Matt's voice, as though anything I said evoked his contempt. My questions or attempts at simple pleasantries were met with a scowl and an irritated response or—worse—silence.

"What's your schedule today?" I gently attempted to check in.

"Why? I've got clients back-to-back all day long," he almost spat back.

"I just wanted to know your schedule. You don't have to jump down my throat."

He responded in his most reasonable voice, denying any ill feeling, "All I said is I am very busy today."

I retreated in hurt silence, becoming more guarded about sharing my feelings of sadness, loneliness, and fear.

Matt and I would both turn 45 that year, which felt like a seismic midlife shift to me—a critical time to take stock and make course corrections about the direction of our lives. Matt seemed agitated, maybe restless, which I took to be a good sign. I was hoping this was his growth edge, a challenge that would lead to positive change. He seemed to be operating on a track, diligently moving along with a goal in mind. I was wanting to look around, explore, take the scenic route, and perhaps take a major detour.

My restlessness had begun a few years earlier, an upwelling from deep within. We were active in our church community, and I was participating in a prayer and discussion group. One evening the group leader posed the question, "When have you felt the love of God?" The question left me a little cold. I could not immediately recall instances of divine love embracing me. I was disturbed by my inability to relate to what felt like an essential aspect of my faith journey. I began to seriously question my understanding of God. Growing up with the image of a patriarchal God the Father, judgmental and punitive, I hadn't felt trusting or intimate with God. Perhaps it was time for me to explore a more grown-up spirituality.

I often woke in the wee hours of the morning between 2:00 and 4:00 a.m. If sleep eluded me, I would get up and spend time reading or journaling during these precious stolen hours. One of these early mornings, I intuitively took down a book that had been sitting on my shelf for months. I was amazed to discover images and language of a feminine face of God. My relationship with the Divine was suddenly transformed from the inside out. This seemed totally possible to me; I didn't intellectually believe God was gendered at all. If God could be imagined as female, I could truly be made in Her image. I felt a rush of deep affirmation. Perhaps this was the love of God. I was captivated by this new exploration and even wished that the world could stop for a while so I could immerse myself in study and prayer.

As apparent fulfillment of the adage *Be careful what you wish for*, within a few months, I became seriously ill. I lost weight quickly, was unable to eat, and felt easily sapped of strength. It took a few months of tests before I was diagnosed with a fist-size tumor in my belly. By then, I was so thin and frail, I could actually see the lump bulging in my abdomen. It required immediate surgery and a two-month period of rest and recovery afterward. We scheduled the surgery for a week after the diagnosis to allow the doctors to confer and prepare for what they expected to be a complex operation. I felt confident that I would survive the surgery; my surgeon had assured me, "If this was cancer, you'd be dead by now." Still, as I waited those long days and longer nights, my physical frailty and the prospect of major surgery gave rise to middle-of-the-night worries about my mortality and a serious review of my life choices.

In the middle of one night, as I sat in the rocker and tried to soothe my worries, an image came to me of a ring of fire. It was not quite a dream, more a half-waking vision of a huge flaming hoop like I'd seen in the circus, held aloft for a lion or tiger to pass through. I realized that I had to go through the fire—the surgery. I would survive but would be transformed in some essential way. The image comforted and also challenged me. When Matt and I celebrated our 20th anniversary two years later, we chose "Through the Fire" by Chaka Khan for our first dance. Although we did not make a conscious connection to my vision of the ring of fire, there would be more fires—more changes—to come.

The surgery went well, and, thankfully, the tumor was benign. After a week in the hospital, I was discharged to home for my unintended sabbatical. I took time during lucid periods of my recovery to cultivate new interests—feminist spirituality, depth psychology, dream work. As I regained my health and resumed my old life of legal work and family obligations, I reserved time during the week for these new explorations, which fed my soul. While awaiting surgery, I had promised myself to attend to the urgency of living each moment fully and to embrace these new interests. I felt uncomfortable in my own skin, ready to molt. I needed to shed so I could find a new, tender, fresh skin.

These feelings percolated under the surface during the three years between my surgery and the late winter of our 21st year, fed by my extracurricular explorations and eventually demanding more awareness and attention. Sitting together in the family room one evening, I tried sharing my feelings with Matt.

"Don't you ever feel like 'what am I doing?' Like there must be something more that I am called to do beyond this work? I just don't know that I can keep doing this same thing for another 20 years."

"No," he answered, looking up from his laptop. "We are at the peak of our careers and earning potential. In fact," he said, attempting to engage me in planning mode, "if we can both increase our productivity and push through for another 10 years, we will be able to retire. This is not the time to think about stopping or even slowing down. These are the most productive years of our lives."

I didn't want to argue, but I felt like my needs didn't register at all with him. He was striving for the financial finish line. Not only did I *not* have the finish line in mind, I didn't even want to be in the race. I had been running, achieving, and performing for so long. I was exhausted. I craved a rest, in which I could attend to my deepest self, not the one I wore in the world. Matt was in a completely different mode—expanding in the world. He had found a professional groove that took him further outside of himself. He was seeking to don more regalia as I sought to shed mine.

Whenever I would try to share my need to engage in more soulful work, he became anxious and resistant. I would barely get the words out, "Don't you think...?" before he barked, "No." He was afraid—and perhaps not unreasonably so—that I would decide to stop working, which would have left the financial heavy lifting to him. Although we both worked hard and similar hours, as a lawyer, I had always made more money and been the primary earner in our partnership. If I were to slow down or change my career, it would have a significant impact on our finances.

He couldn't indulge my whimsy if it threatened our whole family structure. We seemed unable to have a constructive conversation about my need for change and his need for stability and predictability. I enthusiastically continued my explorations but became more protective of the tender aspects of my new growth and less willing to trust Matt to respond sensitively to my sharing.

I often joked that Matt "gave at the office," the old pat response to the doorbell solicitation for donations. But I wasn't talking about financial contributions. Matt was a dedicated professional, and he gave himself fully to his work. In addition to his years of psychology training, he had a natural well of empathy—an ability to truly see and receive another person in the depth of their suffering. I have often seen him with tears brimming as he recalled a client's pain. When he got home at the end of a long day, he was not always interested in conversation or emotional engagement.

My tendency was the opposite. I wanted to report all the drama of the work day, my frustrations and strokes of brilliance, while he often listened in silence. I needed engagement to work through my own feelings. I paid a therapist to listen and help me reflect on my experience, while my husband was consumed by listening to others. I wanted him to turn that empathic gaze toward me.

Matt seemed to feel I was less available in the marriage as well, complaining when I was heading off to a meeting or dreamwork session. Following my surgery, I had cultivated new interests, beginning depth therapy, dreamwork, and an exploration of women, law, and spirituality with three other women. That spring, I was offering my first women's spiritual retreat over the six weeks of Lent, a reflective period before Easter. I had also started teaching a course on the theology of marriage at Santa Clara University. I tried to keep my new commitments to daytime hours, stealing time from my work day. But I would occasionally be away in the evenings, missing dinner and leaving him alone to handle homework or whatever the kids might need. He could sense that I was pulling away from him. I felt like he had been emotionally unavailable to me for a long while because of his work and his fears about what my changes might mean for him. I wanted to talk through these differences, but it seemed he was either too tired, preoccupied, or just not open to hearing about my growing discontent.

We had been together a long time at this point. We had shared many life changes in building our family and both of our careers. Matt and I married young, only a few years out of college. We were both still students—me in law school and Matt in graduate school. We had Tyler right away, and four years later, we welcomed our daughter, Cassedy, naming her with my last name and Matt's surname. We loaded ourselves with responsibility that weighed heavily on our young marriage. With new professional degrees and two small children, we returned to our native California, diving into a full-time work-and-family juggling act. Into that busy life, we welcomed our third child, Timothy. The next decade was consumed with developing careers, raising three children, a full plate of community involvements, and both of our extended families. We had just celebrated 20 years of navigating these changes together. But this midlife transition felt different. While the earlier transitions were about building something together, this felt like things potentially coming apart.

21st year, Sunday afternoon

Late one afternoon, the air fresh with recent rain and the sun dimly shining, I managed to sneak away for a run alone through the neighborhood park. As I jogged along, my mind loosened a bit, falling into rhythm with the steady motion of my steps. I replayed the conversation I wanted to have with Matt about our future. Why was it so hard for him to hear my unrest? I supposed I was not hearing his anxieties about work and financial security either. It just seemed like the goal line kept moving, always just a little bit more. Running along, I began to see how easily we became defensive with each other.

I felt like another person was brewing inside of me, wanting to come forward but stifled by my career and family responsibilities. I felt Matt's anger coming through in our conversations and could imagine he was feeling some of the same frustration and reluctance to open up to me as I felt with him. We both harbored wounds that festered in the dark. When we could have risked sharing and reaching out to each other, we retreated instead. We reminded ourselves that it wasn't safe. I could see we needed to do some serious work to get rid of those hurts—to expose them, clean them out, and let them heal. Then we needed to build trust again. It wouldn't be easy, but I believed it would be worthwhile. Perhaps we needed to work with a therapist, although we had never been to formal counseling before. Maybe this midlife juncture was the time to deal with our old wounds and hurtful patterns, to reset for the second half of life. I envisioned years of couple's therapy, dredging up all the old disappointments we were each carrying, purging them through long emotional conversations, and eventually letting them go. As I ran, I could feel the weight of it in my body with each step; it felt like so much work. Wouldn't it be great if we could just start fresh, let go of all the baggage, and see each other anew? But relationships, especially marriages, don't tend to work that way.

I knew ours was a good marriage that had just grown tired, dry, and uninspired. There is drudgery even in a very good marriage. The monotony of day-to-day tasks can drain it of its vitality. Tensions around finances, children, and work that we each bring home slowly grind against the higher values of love, family, and security. The rough edges are worn away like river stones tumbling against one another for years, meeting and eroding each other's resistance and uniqueness. We get stuck, we get bored, we cling to our patterns of behavior out of fear and plain exhaustion. The container becomes an old shoe—worn, scuffed around the edges, and beat. How do we rekindle the spark, revitalize the deeper commitment?

There is drudgery even in a very good marriage. The monotony of day-to-day tasks can drain the vitality out of the marriage. Tension around finances, children, and work stresses that we each bring home slowly grind against the higher values of love, family, and security.

Reflection

- What are my dreams? Does our partnership support my dreams?
- Do I support my partner's dreams for their own future?
- What conversations and compromises might we need to have about how we are feeling with our current life, balance, and dreams for the future?
- How can we best hold those conversations so that we both feel comfortable to share?

4

FANTASY

Sunday afternoon

Coming home from my solitary run, physically tired but emotionally invigorated, I headed to the kitchen for a drink. Matt's long body was draped over the kitchen counter, his ear phones dangling, as he listened intently and took notes. I poured myself a glass of cold water and leaned against the opposite counter, inviting conversation. He paused the recording to check in.

"Hey. How was your run?"

"Nice. It felt good to get out and loosen up a bit," I answered. "What are you listening to?"

"Oh, this psychologist talking about marriage. Kind of interesting. He says fantasy and play are necessary for a long-term love relationship to thrive." He raised his eyebrow teasingly.

I detected this not-so-subtle hint that I wasn't playing along. Straightening, I defended myself from the perceived attack, challenging the authorities, "Whose definition of fantasy?"

"Hey, calm down. I'm just saying that this marriage expert thinks that, in order to survive, a marriage needs a sense of play or fantasy or fun. What's wrong with that?"

"So, who decides what is playful? Whose definition of fun?" I huffed off for the shower, finishing over my shoulder, "Seems to me like one of those male fantasy claims to put women on the defensive: 'Can't you take a joke?'—when it's not funny at all. The same old thing."

This touched off our classic dance around intimacy and sexuality. For me, our deep heart connection was the necessary foundation for sexual intimacy. For Matt, sexual intimacy cultivated and opened the way to deep emotional sharing.

Sexuality had always been uncertain ground for me—intriguing but filled with hidden hazards. As the second of four daughters, my childhood household was hugely feminine; even the cats were female. My sisters and I were active and adventurous tomboys and then got out our dolls to play house and dress-up games. I never viewed femininity as a limitation; it seemed to me to be a great plus. I could do everything boys could do and also be creative, nurturing, and emotional—qualities more permissible for girls. I enjoyed the strength and athleticism of my young body, full of possibility.

We attended Catholic grade school taught by Notre Dame nuns, powerful women dressed in traditional habits, with all signs of femininity buried under layers of black veils from head to toe. The nuns were important role models for me as a smart, ambitious girl. I saw that women could be intelligent, competent, and powerful, but it seemed to be at the price of femininity and sexuality. As I began my growth into womanhood, I felt the sting of shame around menstruation, budding sexuality, and desire. I associated sexuality with shame and female sexuality with submission and a loss of personal power.

In college, I excitedly joined the emergent feminist movement of the 1970s, finding expression for the capable, independent woman I aspired to become. I understood feminism to be my right to cultivate qualities and participate in activities, whether considered masculine or feminine by the patriarchal culture. But even within this women's political movement, I felt that my femininity—the part of me that enjoyed attention from boys, as well as primping, shaving, and curling rituals—was unacceptable and needed to be kept hidden. Masculine clothing, boots, and unshaven legs seemed to be proof of dedication to the cause. Again, empowerment seemed to require a sacrifice of femininity. The personal was political. My feminism demanded that I live out my relationships with uncompromising integrity, and I chose empowerment over femininity.

I brought the shame of my sexuality and the seriousness of my feminist politics to our marriage. Certainly, lovemaking was enjoyable, but never frivolous or wanton. I always preferred the term *lovemaking* to *having sex*, which sounded so transactional. Lovemaking spoke to the larger context of intimacy, a part of which was sexual, but all held within the sanctity of marriage. You could say I was kind of sanctimonious about our sex life.

In the early 1980s, when I began my legal work, women were entering the law in large numbers, but the profession was still very much defined and dominated by men. The expectations of dress for women lawyers at that time demonstrated this tension. Women lawyers were to dress plainly—asexually, really—in a blue, black, or gray suit with a white blouse buttoned to the neck and tied up with a bow. It was not so different from our Catholic school uniforms. We were allowed no jewelry except classic pearls and no noticeable makeup. Our hair was either cut very short or pulled up in a schoolmarm's bun. Ironically, though, women lawyers also had to wear skirts, to show a little leg. Everything in the uniform was designed to neutralize any feminine appearance, but we were also to be readily identifiable as female by the skirt.

In our first years of marriage, like many law students, I worked full-time for law firms during the summers. I would put on my uniform each morning, squelching any overt signs of femininity—much less sexuality—to go out into the world. In the law office, I had the disembodied experience of being a capable and dedicated contributor while denying any personal or family needs so as not to draw attention to my femaleness. Coming home each night, I would shed the uniform and try to climb back into my marriage to become a wife and young mother. Struggling with this divide, the tension was visceral. I remember seriously considering asking Matt whether we could maybe just postpone our sexual relationship during those summer months while I worked in law firms. I never did, but I lived this contradiction between what it meant to be a strong, professional woman and what it meant to be a wife.

I found a way in the marriage to be sexually responsive and

receptive but not explicitly aggressive or initiatory. I navigated an understanding between Catholicism, feminism, and patriarchy that allowed sexual enjoyment within the sanctity of marriage. Still, all of these influences of the personal as political kept that sexuality in a carefully constructed box, with lots of rules for myself.

Thankfully, Matt had a healthy appetite and approach to sex. He just plain enjoyed it. He had been an athlete—a swimmer—all his life and was very comfortable in his own skin, in his body—and in mine. He took the lead early on and was not going to let me hide my sexuality in a closet somewhere. He would sometimes tell me that sex was a "barometer of the marriage." As goes the sexual relationship, so goes the entire marriage, he warned.

That felt to me like a psychologist's manipulative challenge—paradoxical or reverse psychology, heavily laden with judgment. I didn't agree that sex was the ultimate measure of the marriage. For me, the crux of the marriage was our emotional connection and intimacy, from which the lovemaking would naturally develop. In other words, emotional intimacy became a prerequisite to our sexual encounter. For him, the sexual engagement provided the intimacy and healing to open the emotional connection.

We had done this dance for over two decades. He would initiate, invite, or hint at a sexual rendezvous. My response was usually based on how emotionally connected I felt and whether we had found time for intentional conversation or even simple affection. But affection had become a hazardous middle ground between sexual and emotional intimacy that we were both hesitant to enter. Over time, my resistance softened as I found healing in our sexual intimacy. It was loving and intimate, vulnerable and connected. In the afterglow, my husband's heart and soul opened and invited me in. The emotional intimacy that I tried to insist upon as a prerequisite flowed naturally as a by-product. I began to trust the depth of our intimacy and fidelity, which allowed greater trust and sharing.

With the demands of family and work, sex could become routine, sometimes almost obligatory. When a couple who had been long-time friends of ours decided to separate, the wife confided to me that they had not had sex for years. I was surprised and saddened. They were both vibrant, attractive young people. She also shared how hard it was to even make the approach after such a long time.

I made another rule for myself: We would have sex, maybe even make love, at least once a week, no matter what. Sometimes that meant making love in the middle of the night, after falling exhausted into bed and before rising with an early alarm to begin the day's routine. Sometimes it meant a leisurely Sunday afternoon when we found ourselves child-free for an hour or two. But there was always a baseline, a minimum guarantee. It was sometimes more practice than passion, but it was sustainable and, thankfully, was punctuated by more intentional and intimate encounters.

Even as I struggled with the many pulls on my own sexual identity, I realized it was time to engage our daughter in this conversation. At age 15, Cassedy was becoming serious about her first boyfriend. She had avoided the boy craze of middle school, which, when compared with her sports and actual drama activities, seemed to her like a waste of energy. By the time she entered high school, she was ready to explore this new territory. Even at her young age, she had a self-confident lightness about her, not taking herself too seriously but always concerned and engaged on behalf of her friends. She was fresh and spontaneous, and I wanted so much for this first experience with romance to be fun and caring for her.

When I was her age, I felt that my mother had utterly failed me. As I began sexual explorations with boyfriends, my mother was silent. I didn't ask, but she sure didn't tell, which seemed to me to be her responsibility. I blamed her for my missteps, for those awkward and hurtful early experiences I stumbled through without guidance. I tripped many times over how to handle pressure from boys, how to set boundaries, and how to walk that narrow line between being "loose" and being a "tease." Although the language changes with each generation, the question persists: How do you remain true to yourself while also engaging in and exploring new relationships? I promised myself I would do better by my daughter when the time came. I wanted her to be informed and empowered in her relationships—and to know she could turn to me.

Although Cassedy and I enjoyed open communication, I was concerned whether she would feel comfortable to share with me about this tender topic. I recalled attending a parent meeting offered through Tyler's after-school childcare program several years earlier when he was finishing elementary school: "How to talk to your kids about sex." Every parent was there, desperate for advice. It was an entertaining evening, and I learned a lot. Certain pieces of advice were contrary to my instincts but made a lot of sense, and I was glad for the instruction. First, the instructor advised us anxious parents not to begin this conversation with scare tactics about the risks of STDs or pregnancy. I had thought that would be a great starting place. So, what then?

"Start by talking about love," she said. *Ahhh*s rose up among the audience.

She also debunked the idea that our children would ask about sex when they were ready.

"They will never ask," she told us. "Kids have gotten the clear message over time that sex is a taboo topic, and they are unlikely to initiate this conversation." There went another of my strategies.

I wanted my daughter to have good information and support around her budding sexuality, and I realized it was up to me to initiate this conversation. It was time. Cassedy and I had gone out for a long walk that early winter, as we often did. It seemed like a good time to raise the subject.

"Cass, it seems you and Adam are getting more serious, and I just want you to know that I was once your age. I've been there. I didn't feel that Gramma told me things I needed to know about relationships with boys and especially about sex. I want you to know that I am here, and I'm happy to talk with you any time about any questions you might have or anything you want to talk about."

Satisfied that I had made the invitation, we walked a little farther.

"Okay, Mom," she blurted, "I don't know anything about sex, so why don't you just tell me everything."

I stumbled in my tracks. She was serious. I was not prepared to go beyond my gracious opening, but I quickly put my thoughts in order, trying to remember the instructor's sage advice from all those years earlier. I don't remember exactly where I started or what I said. I tried to talk about love, but I'm not sure I connected on that score. It seemed like an evasion, and I wanted to make good on my promise to share with her honestly about sex. I fumbled around, talking about touching and feelings, different kinds of sexual activity, and logistics.

Pausing to take a breath and reflect on what I most wanted to say, what I wanted for my daughter, I continued. "I want you to feel comfortable in your body and with your sexuality. I want you to be able to claim sexuality on your own terms, enjoy yourself, and feel empowered not to do anything you don't want to do. I want you to become a proud, sensitive, self-possessed woman."

I was surprised listening to myself. I thought information was what I had wanted from my mother in my teen years, but it turned out that I was really looking for a vision of womanhood that was sensual, self-possessed, and alive to the world. Until that moment, I hadn't realized that this image of womanhood was what I needed in my life but had so far been unable to articulate. If I could envision the possibility for her, perhaps I could create this same possibility for myself. Cassedy was listening intently and, I realized, was probably overwhelmed. I laughed and added, "Once you figure it out, come teach me."

We walked a long way farther in silence, leaving the conversation open to take up again and again over the next many months. Not only had I given my daughter the support I had so wanted for myself at her age, but I had also created a vision for both of us of a conscious feminine sexuality not much present in our culture.

I remembered this conversation as I reflected on Matt's virtual marriage guru's advice about fantasy and play in the marriage. I could see how Matt's more spontaneous, more playful desires rubbed up against the edge of my sanctimonious approach to sex. Was there a way to reconcile these feelings? How could I claim my sexuality within the confines I had imposed on myself and on our marriage? How could we shift years-long patterns?

We had three children, the first off to college already, but our teenage daughter and 11-year-old son still demanded our daily attention.

It was a critical time in Matt's work in the world. He was trying to not only make the most of it financially but also to leave his mark in the field—to establish his reputation for professional excellence and build his legacy. He also saw it as a time to enjoy good health, physical strength, and vitality, as he could see that these would soon begin to fade. When he thought of fantasy, what did that mean for him? I had been too busy arguing against it to ask, but somewhere deep inside, a light switched on.

> *What I was looking for was a vision of womanhood—sensual, self-possessed, alive to the world. If I could envision the possibility for my daughter, perhaps I could create this same possibility for myself.*

Reflection

- How do I feel about fantasy or play in our intimate life?
- Do I relate to the tension between emotional and sexual intimacy? What is that tension and how does it manifest in our relationship?
- What rules have I created for my sexual self? For our sexual relationship?

5

BALANCING DREAMS

Monday evening

The evening after our conversation about fantasy, I arrived home after a full day at the office and launched right into family dinner and homework. When I climbed into bed, I was ready to unplug and drop into my bedside reading. We had purchased our small home several years earlier and, over time, had remodeled it, adding on so that each child had their own room and Matt had his own office. I realized at one point that while everyone else in the family had a room of their own, the only private space I had in the house was my side of the bed. When I climbed into it, surrounded by my books and journal, it was my refuge, my personal retreat.

Despite our underlying tensions, Matt and I had an easy rhythm in the evenings. We both enjoyed time to wind down before bed—but not that night. He was distraught about the strange voicemail he had received that day and insistently interrupted to share it with me. I took the phone and listened.

"Hello, Dr. Sullivan. This is your secret admirer. I've been watching you, and I'm hoping we can get together real soon. Bye."

The secret admirer's voice was feminine, teasing, inviting.

"I've listened to it over and over, and I can't figure out who it is."

Was he just testing me? It was clearly my voice. Did he really not recognize it? I searched his face, but he showed no sign of recognition.

"What if it's a client or an opposing party? Or just someone who wants to lure me into a trap?"

I wasn't sure how to respond. I was surprised by Matt's distress and almost paranoid reaction. It was just a phone message, but he was imagining all kinds of nefarious motives. He paced back and forth in front of the bed, continuing to imagine an evil conspiracy.

"Honey, it's probably nothing. You haven't done anything wrong, and there's really nothing you can do right now anyway," I tried. "Come on. Calm down. Come to bed, and we'll just see what happens."

I watched him distractedly get ready for bed, slowly letting the urgency go. I was a little stirred up myself, wondering what this might bring. He didn't recognize my voice, but I was glad he had shared the message with me rather than stressing about it privately. He could be so intense and serious but also so sensitive. I loved his willingness to be emotionally vulnerable with me, to open up and trust me. Beneath our surface tensions, we had a solid partnership and had built an abundant life together.

Our days were full. Matt and I usually woke early to head to the gym or out for a run through the neighborhood park before the kids woke up. Then the morning hustle began with making coffee, getting breakfast for the kids, assembling lunches, checking homework, and organizing game schedules and uniforms. Then we were off driving kids to school and ourselves to offices or courtrooms. Our oldest, Tyler, was away at college in San Diego, playing baseball and living near the beach. We tried to get away at least once a month to visit him and watch a couple of his games. Cassedy was in the throes of high school—sports, studies, girlfriends, and now the boyfriend. Our youngest, Timmy, at age 11, was already busy with soccer, school, and friends. We were also involved with our large extended family, several grandparents, and even a great-grandma.

Matt and I both had full-on careers, demanding our focused engagement during the work week. We were active in our local church community, serving as lectors on Sundays, as well as teaching and working with the leadership of our parish. Then we had our respective professional organizations with evening meetings and continuing education requirements. Add to all that managing a household, bills, and repairs, on top of planning a kitchen remodel. And that was on a good day, when no one got sick or broke an arm or forgot their shin guards or lost a best friend. I often wondered how people did it single-handedly. Separated or divorced parents, even if both are involved with the children during the course of a week, are single-parenting on a daily basis, handling all the logistics alone. We not only shared these responsibilities with each other, but we also had two grandmas and an amazing auntie nearby to fill the gaps when we couldn't.

Equal partnership had been an early agreement and ethic in our marriage. In fact, the idea of equality had its roots in our relationship long before we were married. We both had the opportunity to attend college at Stanford University, Matt on a swimming scholarship and me as a bright public-school kid from San Jose also on scholarship. We met, appropriately enough, in the Human Biology Program. In the spring of our junior year, we began working together on a health policy course, Matt from the health side, my focus more on policy. I had been selected by our department chair as the head teaching assistant (TA) to lead the capstone policy course and was charged with recruiting nine other TAs from our student ranks to develop the course materials and facilitate student task forces. A mutual friend suggested I interview Matt to join the team. Thankfully, I did and then hired him.

I recognized Matt vaguely from our core human biology courses and from around campus. He was a swimmer, and I would occasionally see him hanging out with other athletes—part of the cool crowd, which I was not. We met for the interview at the campus coffee shop. Matt was casual, in faded jeans and a flannel shirt. He was quiet and veiled, with shoulder-length waves of curls, tinted glasses shading his dreamy blue eyes, and a full, burly, red-tinged beard. He was mysterious, and I was intrigued but not attracted. As we got to know each other, I respected his guarded privacy, knowing he was going through a breakup with his longtime girlfriend. But I shared freely with him about myself, my communication problems with my longtime boyfriend, and my enthusiasm for our joint project. We worked side by side through the summer and fall months of our senior year, preparing the course, researching and gathering materials, planning lectures and guest panelists, and coordinating the 200 students into task forces to work on the selected policy issues focused on reproductive health, including access to contraception and funding for abortion. We literally wrote a book on birth control.

At first, Matt and I were competitive with each other, trying to keep up with what the other had read and trading ideas for the project. We quickly grew into a strong team, with me in the lead and him reliably at my side. Matt had recently quit the swim team and was renewing his academic commitment. I was focused on organizing the many aspects of the course and fulfilling my responsibility to pull it all together. I chaired the meetings of our team, 4 professors and 10 TAs, including one intimidating emeritus professor. It was a daunting task, but it was manageable because I knew I could turn to Matt when needed for information or support.

Late in our year of working together, Matt arrived at a holiday gathering with a clean-shaven face. Without the bushy beard, the shape and tenderness of his face came into view—soft cheeks, strong jaw, and full lips. I was a little stunned and stirred. His face was suddenly expressive, coyly smiling or ponderously frowning. Around the holiday table with other students and staff, he seemed to be flirting with me, teasing and smiling with his now visible face. I felt his attention like static electricity between us. I was flattered and flustered. We had been working together for months without any sign of attraction. I trusted him and knew he respected me, but, to my surprise, a new conversation was happening.

The next morning, I gathered my books to rush out for class. When I opened my dorm room door into the hallway, I found a sweet flower with a poem written in Matt's recognizable all-caps printing. I was tickled by this new flirtation. The possibility of building a romantic connection on a foundation of mutual respect and shared responsibility was surprising and something I had only hoped might be possible in a love relationship—a true partnership.

A few days later, Matt asked if I liked to ski and mentioned he would be spending a few days during our Christmas break at his family's cabin in Lake Tahoe. Yes, I liked to ski, but I was more intrigued by the possibility of a romantic getaway. He picked me up at my family's home in San Jose a couple days after Christmas, and we drove the several hours to Lake Tahoe. We spent three days together skiing, yes, but also talking, laughing, playing in the snow, and cuddling up in front of the fire. We drove back on New Year's Eve and continued our romantic engagement through the rest of our holiday break.

Our policy course was beginning in January, and, as we returned to campus, we kept our new relationship a secret from the other TAs and students—or so we thought. Perhaps I was concerned about undermining my own authority as the lead TA for the program, or maybe I didn't want to burst the bubble of this surprising love affair. Others recognized the spark between us, and soon we were out as a couple. Continuing to work on the policy course and then completing our college coursework, I delighted in Matt's attention and connection, but questions about our future loomed unspoken.

Matt was planning a career in medicine. His father was a doctor, and, as the youngest of his four children, Matt was taking on the mantle to follow in his father's footsteps. His mother, trained as a nurse, had stayed home to take care of the children and the home. Matt had grown up with this traditional model of marriage, which seemed perfectly acceptable to him.

My parents also had a traditional marriage in terms of roles, although my father's schedule as a commercial airline pilot was far from normal. He would be gone for days and then home midweek for several days in a row. My mother was responsible for the household and their four daughters. She had been trained as a teacher but had never worked outside the home. Unlike Matt, I rejected this sex-role arrangement as a model for my marriage and family. I expected to use my skills and education to be a force in the world. I also wanted to have a family but was not sure it was possible to do both.

In my women's history course, I learned that many accomplished women suffered the epitaph "But she never married" or "She had no children." This struck me as an unfair detraction from the women's contributions; men's marital or family status was not deemed essential to their legacy. It also implied that family life was the price for a woman's work in the world. I rejected the false choice of sacrificing family life for meaningful work. A balance between work and family was an essential priority for me and, as you will see, a formative element of our marriage.

Although I didn't have a clear plan about my career, it was critical to me to figure out how I could combine my work with the family I wanted to have. I had the good fortune to take a course at Stanford on the psychology of sex roles from Daryl and Sandra Bem, a then-husband-and-wife team who taught a model of egalitarian marriage, including what they had learned in their own partnership. The course was full of practical advice about nonsexist child rearing, the politics and practicalities of shared housework, and the economics and psychology of equal partnership in marriage. I was sold.

At one point, I touted my newfound liberation to my mother. I was home from college for a visit when she made an offhand comment about women giving up their "maiden" names when they married. I immediately retorted that I was not going to change my name for any man.

"If you're not ready to take a man's name, then you're not ready to be married," she warned.

"I am not going to take his name unless he takes my name. And," I continued, making a pointed reference to her and my father, "If he doesn't wear a wedding ring, I won't wear one either."

Surprised and probably sincerely concerned for my future, she scolded, "You'll never find a man who will put up with that!"

"Then I guess I won't get married!" I said, and I meant it. Equality in a relationship felt essential to me.

I also introduced this discussion with Matt early in our relationship, sharing what I thought was a stroke of brilliance for balancing work and family.

"If both parents work part time, they could both have careers and both participate in raising their children."

He immediately dismissed the idea. "I am going to be too busy saving the world to take care of children. That will be my wife's job."

At least that's what I remember him saying.

"So, you don't even know who you are going to marry, but you already know that your work is more important than her work?" I challenged, feeling brilliant.

"Yeeeah," he said, drawing out the affirmative as though it were a foregone conclusion. I guess, for him, it was. This might have cooled my interest in pursuing our relationship, but I had seen how we worked together, how he respected and supported me. I held out hope that he might eventually see the value in sharing work and family roles.

We both spent the next year working and planning for our next steps: law school for me and medical school for Matt. Matt broke up with me briefly during the year, feeling that he needed to focus on his own path. I ultimately persuaded him that our relationship need not interfere with his plans. It could be a support and even accelerator of his dreams. Together, we were stronger and could accomplish more than either of us could alone. As we continued our relationship and formed our career plans, Matt felt my support and also saw my commitment to my own work. He was slowly coming around to the idea that we could each build meaningful careers and both be present for a family.

Through a series of twists and turns that I will return to, we were married about two years later. Once Matt laid eyes on our infant son, he was fully committed to equal parenting. We were both full-time students when Tyler was born, me in law school and Matt in his psychology doctoral program. Although we didn't have any money, we had time and flexibility to share childcare responsibilities. We also didn't have the pressure that many new parents have of one partner's income being more essential, leveraging the decision of how to divide work and family roles. We shared everything equally. I put the baby to bed one night, and he did it the next night. We alternated diaper changes and feedings after I stopped nursing.

We shared laundry duty and cleaned our apartment together on Saturday mornings. One thing that wasn't equal was cooking; Matt did the cooking. I loved to bake, but it didn't balance making dinner every night, even though I did always clean up afterward.

I was concerned about this imbalance in our contributions and decided I needed to step up on the kitchen front. I committed as a New Year's resolution to make dinner one night a week for the entire year. It was not exactly equal, but it would break the pattern of his cooking and my cleaning. By then, I had graduated from law school and was working full time on Capitol Hill. I worked for the Congressional Caucus for Women's Issues on various legislative initiatives, including drafting the first Family Leave Act. Matt was finishing his coursework in psychology and had begun work on his dissertation. He still did all the shopping and prepared the meals most nights. But as promised, on Tuesday nights, I returned home from work, tired, and rummaged around our apartment's tiny kitchen to see what I could muster into some semblance of a meal. A couple of problems immediately became evident. One, I hated cooking. Two, I was not good at it. Three, I wasn't prepared. Trying to be helpful, Matt would hover around the small kitchen, making infuriating suggestions. We both knew he could do it better and faster and that the resulting meal would be tastier, which only made it more frustrating for both of us. By the time we sat down to eat whatever I had cooked up, I was usually angry, and the food was far from delicious. Adding to the tension, Matt had to get up and clean the kitchen after dinner, which he hated.

It was a disaster from the start, and although it never really got any better, we stuck it out for the entire year. But that was the end of that. We learned that equal didn't have to be absolutely identical. It could be reciprocal and balanced. As long as we both agreed to the trade-offs, it was fair and fine. You cook, and I clean? No problem! You handle the cars, and I pay the bills? Done! You clean the toilets, and I do the laundry? Absolutely! Eventually, we each had our domains and were glad for the other's contributions. We could share responsibilities and specialize. We also dared not criticize how the other did their jobs. Our shared motto of "If you don't like it, do it yourself" kept us each quite content with the way the other did their chores.

This egalitarian aspect was central to our partnership and carried over to our intimacy. Our relationship, sexual and otherwise, didn't need to be absolutely equal; it did need to balance out over time. Our relationship was more about mutuality, receptivity to the other, and reciprocity. *Equality* implies a rigid and quantitative situation. *Mutuality* conjures a flow over time. It implies responsibility and availability, but allows differing contributions, depending on each of our preferences and outside obligations at any point in time. It was okay to settle into roles like cooking and cleaning, initiating and receiving, so long as we each were content with the balance. This understanding gave us greater freedom to find a rhythm that worked for us.

Eventually, this reciprocity allowed us to support each other and also to lean on one another. Neither of us was ever very good at asking for help, but I knew—and was deeply grateful knowing—that, if I needed to fall apart, Matt could hold me until I could gather myself again. I could also be his strength and support when he needed it. Trusting in this mutual support became crucial for each of us during times of personal challenges.

My illness and eventual surgery in my early 40s was a good example. We had both been pushing and striving in work and equally involved at home, when I was suddenly unable to hold up my end. I was disabled by pain, weakness, and paralyzing fatigue. I couldn't work more than a half day and came home utterly exhausted. Matt had to take up the slack at home, continue his own work commitments, and take care of me in new ways before and after the surgery as my strength slowly returned. He shouldered the additional responsibilities and also called on family and friends for support to see us through until I could regain my strength.

After recovering from the surgery, I returned to work and, at the same time, sought to expand into new ways of working with marriage. I hoped to apply what I was learning through divorce work to support healthy marriages. I was delighted when I was invited to teach an undergraduate course in the Religious Studies Department at Santa Clara University titled "Theology of Marriage." I had audited the course during my recovery, began teaching the next semester, and continued for about five years. To my surprise, I was given wide latitude in framing the curriculum. I laid a foundation of the traditional teachings about marriage, as well as an anthropological view from my human biology background. But I then steered the course in a more practical direction, encouraging students to think consciously about—and prepare for—their future partnerships.

I assigned *The Good Marriage* by Judith Wallerstein and Sandra Blakeslee as the primary text and framework for the class. Wallerstein was a premier psychologist and divorce researcher at the time, best known for her 25-year longitudinal study (1975–2000) on the effects of divorce on children. I appreciated her desire as a long-married divorce professional to make a positive contribution to marriage. *The Good Marriage* was based on extended interviews with 50 couples who met her criteria for a happy marriage as well as her extensive work with couples and her own long-standing marriage. The couples selected were drawn from her home base north of San Francisco Bay. Although they were a limited sample, their stories offered my students a view into a variety of successful long-term marriages. Her book set out four basic types of marriage and nine essential tasks of a good marriage, providing my students a helpful framework for examining marriage and beginning to envision their own partnerships.

Wallerstein's four types of marriage are romantic, traditional, companionate, and rescue. The romantic marriage is the one we all wish for and are led to believe we will have. It is based on a passionate connection that endures throughout the marriage, almost to the exclusion of others—including the children. Traditional marriage, like those of Matt's and my parents, is defined by the distinct gender roles of homemaker and breadwinner. It has a strong focus on children, almost to the exclusion of the couple. A companionate marriage, like ours, is founded on partnership without prescribed roles but with everything up for negotiation. The rescue marriage she describes arises from a wound to one or both partners. Rescue marriages have the potential to heal prior trauma but also run the risk of reenacting negative patterns and retraumatizing one or both spouses. Of course, marriages may include elements of more than one type and may even change over time. The model offered me a way of evaluating our marriage and focusing on both its strengths and vulnerabilities.

While Matt and I had rejected the traditional model, the companionate marriage had its own benefits and challenges. We were a great team in managing the many tasks of a two-career, three-child family. The risk for a companionate marriage is that, although the partnership may be highly functional, it can come to feel more like a business relationship than a romance. For this type of marriage, I learned that it is especially important to nurture the romantic connection, lest the marriage become dominated by the logistics of managing children, work, and family. This was clearly a risk for us.

Since I was using *The Good Marriage* for my course and Judy Wallerstein lived only an hour away, I invited her to come speak to my students and discuss their questions. Judy was close to 80 years old at the time and had been married for 55 years. After her prepared remarks, she engaged in open conversation with the students. They were all seniors in college, full of questions about how to know when they had met Mr. or Ms. Right, how to stay married, and the essential ingredients of a good marriage. One student asked Judy if she thought a couple could have a good marriage without sex. I may have blushed, but Judy jumped right in.

"No, I don't think so," she said, fairly unequivocally to my surprise. "Perhaps if there were a situation where one of the partners was disabled, I could imagine that, but then they would need to find another form of intimacy. I believe sexual intimacy is an essential aspect of a good marriage."

A hush fell over the students as they took in the wisdom of this octogenarian advocate for marriage.

> ***Our relationship, sexual and otherwise, didn't need to be absolutely equal; it did need to balance out over time.***

Reflection

- What type of marriage did I observe as a child?
- Which of the four models or types of marriage do I have or want to have?
- What are the benefits and potential pitfalls for our model of marriage?
- Do I feel empowered to create the marriage that I want?
- How are roles in our marriage decided? Does gender impact those roles or expectations? What other influences?
- What would I change if I could? What would it take to do so?

Practice

In her book, *The Good Marriage*, Wallerstein sets out nine essential tasks of a good marriage. She likens these tasks of marriage to Erik Erikson's psychosocial developmental tasks of adulthood. Her tasks for a good marriage begin with separation from family of origin and learning to balance autonomy and togetherness. She then moves through other tasks such as welcoming children, coping with crisis, and creating a safe place for conflict. She also emphasizes developing emotional nurturance, sexual intimacy, and laughter. Wallerstein ends with what she terms "double vision," the ability to hold the gaze of the present partner with the remembrance of the younger version.

Judith Wallerstein and Sandra Blakeslee, *The Good Marriage: How and Why Love Lasts* (1996).

- Which of these essential tasks have we worked through?
- Which are stumbling blocks for us?
- Do I agree that they are all essential?

6

DANGEROUS DRIFT

Wednesday night

A couple nights after Matt received the voicemail, we had our usual family dinner, prepared by Matt, and then rushed off to Cassedy's volleyball game. After returning home and tidying up the kitchen, I crawled into bed for my first respite of the day. As I snuggled into my prop of pillows, Matt came in, sat down on the bed, and handed me a folded piece of paper.

"I found this in my car today. In the console," he reported flatly. "I don't know if it was left there while the car was here in the driveway or when I was at the office."

I unfolded the note.

Hi, Doctor Sullivan.

I just love your sexy little car. I've been watching you from afar, and I'm ready to get up close and personal. Leave me your email address so we can communicate.

Can't wait,
Your Secret Admirer

I raised my eyebrows and sighed, meeting his gaze as I handed the note back to him.

"She either knows where I live or where I work! She knows my car! And put a note in it. Who does that?"

Unleashing his anxiety, he went on, "Look at this writing. It's so juvenile. And who writes out *doctor*?" He shook his head.

He was convinced that whoever wrote the note intended him harm in some way, possibly some kind of "honey trap" setup. How sad, I thought, that he didn't believe the attention could simply be because he was an attractive man. He looked back at the note with concern and suspicion. The loopy letters disguised my handwriting, I had thought, and once I was in that playful mindset, it would be natural to spell out *doctor*. As he continued to study the note, I could see a hint of intrigue mixed with the consternation.

"Isn't there some part of this you're enjoying?" I asked.

"Well," he paused. "It is kind of exciting to know that someone is interested and is watching me. I am kind of looking over my shoulder, never knowing if she is watching. Like every woman I see I think, *Is she the one?* It's exciting, but it's also scary. I can see how frightened women who are being stalked must feel. And who is this? I am just afraid it's some client trying to lure me into a trap."

I nodded sympathetically, but there wasn't much I could say. At least he was sharing these contacts with me. I am not naïve about marriage. I do not take our marriage for granted. I know all marriages are vulnerable to erosion and even seduction. I appreciated that he trusted me enough to show me the notes, and I could trust him too. But it did stir things up. Matt climbed into his side of the bed, still distressed and worried, though with some ambivalence. I was also concerned, surprised by his anxiety, wondering whether this secret admirer fantasy might heighten or relieve the tensions between us. We were in a vulnerable place in our marriage. We knew the dangers of allowing distance to grow between us; we had been there before.

Seventh year

We had spent the first five years of our marriage in the Washington, DC, area. I finished law school and spent two years working on Capitol Hill while Matt finished his clinical psychology doctoral program. Once Matt had completed his dissertation, we returned to California with two little kids and two budding careers. We rented a modest home in Palo Alto to be near our families. Matt began an internship at the Palo Alto Veteran's Hospital, where he had worked as a nursing assistant after college. I went to work at a large law firm in San Francisco, which required a two-hour commute each day on top of a demanding work commitment. Matt had more flexibility, so he took primary responsibility for the children, with Tyler starting kindergarten and Cassedy just 9 months old.

I left the house by 6:45 a.m. each morning, usually jogging in my business suit and trainers the few blocks to catch the train to the city, which got me to the office by about 8:15. At night, I caught the 5:35 p.m. express train to walk in the door at 7:00, just in time to sit down for dinner with the family. I sometimes had to work late and would catch the last train, arriving home at 11:00 p.m., to then get up and do it all again the next morning. Matt's program was also demanding, rotating through the various psychology departments and participating in intense training modules with his cohort of about 20 other psychology interns. He was also fully responsible for feeding and clothing both children and getting them to their respective school or care, then picking them up at the end of the day and preparing dinner.

We were both stretched thin and looking for support and appreciation from the other. But we were each too depleted to have much to offer. We had a sort of competition for who was the most taxed, the most exhausted. I would come in the door in the evening, dragging, hoping Matt would acknowledge how tired I was and express his appreciation for my efforts to support our family. Instead, he was looking for me to take some of his load as he tried to manage both kids and get dinner on the table after a full day of juggling his own responsibilities. We weren't willing to give each other a break or even a much-needed pat on the back. We each felt that our share of the load was much heavier.

As we labored, the unthinkable happened. My nine-year-old nephew, Simon, was diagnosed with a brain tumor. My sister, a single mom, was living north of San Francisco with her only child. Simon underwent immediate brain surgery and then started treatments at UC San Francisco. As the nearest family member, I sat with my sister through the surgery, diagnosis, and early treatments. For months, Simon would spend a week in the hospital and then a couple weeks at home before the next round of chemotherapy. The treatments were really tough on this brave little angel. My sister stayed with him in the hospital, and I supported her with visits and meals after work and on weekends. It was heartbreaking to see him suffer and to watch her care for him. It seemed a small offering for me to be with them as much as I possibly could. This created even more separation for Matt and me, as he covered my absences with our own children, and we had less time together than ever.

Matt's internship program was coming to a close and they were hosting a conference for other psychology interns from the Bay Area. It was a week-long conference ending with a party on Saturday evening to close the week and celebrate all of their commencement into practice. I had met the other interns and their partners over the course of the year, although I wasn't very familiar with any of them. Of course, Matt had deep connections with the members of his cohort and had also had an intense week with the other gathered interns. The completion of this formative year was a cause for celebration.

We dropped the kids off with Matt's mom and headed to the party. It was a casual gathering in another intern's rented home. We moved into the easy flow of familiar chatting and high-spirited laughter. The potluck feast was varied and abundant. I finished my generous serving and returned my plate to the small kitchen. Standing at the sink talking with a few people, I suddenly wondered where Matt was. I turned and looked out a large window into the dark of the patio and garden.

My eyes adjusted and found Matt in a full embrace with a female intern. He was facing toward the house, and at just that moment, he looked up and saw me looking at him. It was a moment frozen in time, as we saw in each other's eyes the truth of the embrace. I knew it was not a casual hug but something much more dangerous. He pulled away. I turned around, confused, and starting to smolder with anger. I headed toward the front door, collecting my purse and jacket as I went. Matt quickly found me, and we left with polite goodbyes and awkward silence. Driving home, I was fuming as I waited for him to explain. I didn't think I should have to interrogate him, but he was quiet, which fed my rising anger. *Really?* I thought. *Right now, with all that we are dealing with, this is what is happening?*

When we got back to the house, I walked in and parked myself on the living room sofa, making it clear I was not going to bed until we talked. Matt followed and quietly sat down next to me. While he was the one to usually initiate sexually, it was up to me to begin emotional conversations. I stared silently at the fireplace, boiling with anger, hurt, and confusion.

He took a deep breath and said, "I'm sorry."

He was on edge and attending to my every reaction, but my red-hot stare was not cooling. He admitted the moment was more than friendly. He told me he had been feeling abandoned and alone with my absence, to which I turned my fiery glare on him. I was not going to let this become about me. He continued that he'd been participating in these intense, intimate experiences with the other interns. In one interaction, this young woman had shared emotionally with him, which touched his desire to be needed and his unmet need for deep appreciation. As they shared this emotional connection, he began to feel that she wanted more than friendship, and some part of him wanted that too. Until that moment when our eyes met through the window, he had maybe convinced himself he could get away with it. He assured me nothing had happened. He promised to let her know that there would be nothing more than friendship between them.

I was angry but mostly exhausted. I was deeply disappointed in Matt and annoyed at having to deal with this betrayal when I was already so depleted. I wanted to scream, *Grow up! I'm working myself to the bone to support our family and dealing with life and death issues, and you need to feel needed?* I swallowed the cruel words. I was deeply tired and needed to get some sleep.

As I slowly got ready for bed, my anger began to cool into a mix of other emotions, including relief to have discovered the threat and at the reassurance that Matt was resolved to put an end to it. I trusted him. I remembered another incident when we were living in DC and our Stanford reunion was coming up back in California. We wanted to go, but we had our newborn daughter and four-year-old son to think about, as well as cross-country travel. We had decided that Matt would fly out to California to attend the gathering while I stayed home with the children.

Many of our college friends attended the reunion weekend, most of them unmarried; we were far ahead of the class curve in the marriage and family curriculum. Matt attended an evening event where many very eligible Stanford bachelors were joined by several single women classmates, and one of them set her eyes on him. She and Matt had known each other in college, and perhaps this was unfinished business for her. The story I heard months later was that as the festivities wound down, Matt found himself alone with her, and she offered to sleep with him. This would not have been shocking as college behavior, but Matt was married, with two small children.

Several months later, a letter arrived from this woman we both knew. Matt then told me what had happened, that he had declined her advances, and the letter was her acknowledgment of that. Matt showed me the letter. She referred to their time together at the reunion and said that she respected his "gesture" toward our marriage.

"Gesture!" I blurted. Marital fidelity is more than a gesture. I was shaken by this threat. Our whole marriage and family were hanging in the balance.

Matt apologized for not telling me earlier but assured me nothing had happened, and her letter verified that. The sexual proposition had been uncomfortable for him. While the opportunity for immediate pleasure was inviting, he had realized his marriage and family were on the line and resisted the immediate in favor of the long run. This was a pivotal moment for Matt to realize the depth of his commitment and fidelity. As he had told me then, even if I had never found out, the deceit would have become an obstacle between us. I had good reason to trust him.

But it wasn't quite that simple. A few days after the party, over dinner, five-year-old Tyler said something about the lady they had visited that day.

Eyebrows popping, I asked, "What lady?"

"Daddy's work friend," came the child's innocent response.

I shot Matt an emphatic glare as I stood to clear the table. He gathered the children to get ready for bed. Once we were alone, meeting my demanding silence, he said he had gone to see her but only to put an end to the flirtation.

But he had taken our son and had not told me. Any sympathy I held for his sense of loneliness was quickly disappearing. Although Matt might not have always told me everything, he had never outright lied to me. I trusted him that nothing had happened between them physically, but he was not making good on his promise to end the relationship and was being dishonest about it. I believed he was truly sorry and sincere about ending it, but I needed honest action. I needed to count on him. He vowed that was the end of it.

The internship year soon ended, and the interns all headed off to their new locations. The threatened infidelity faded. In the aftermath, we realized that we had allowed a huge divide to develop between us. In our exhaustion and lack of time together, we had drifted miles apart. We realized that it was not only the threat of conflict and active disagreement that could undermine our marriage. It could also be the inconspicuous, infectious, insidiously slow drift of separate work, separate friends, separate interests until the separate exceeded the joint and the road back together seemed harder than the road apart.

Acclaimed marriage researcher and author John Gottman writes about the ecology of marriage, which resonates with my human biology background. Like the atmosphere or the oceans, he says, "the health of an intimate relationship is an ecosystem." It requires a crucial balance of interactions. Couples need to maintain an overall balance in favor of positive interactions over negative ones. When our interactions dip too much into the negative, love starts to "wither and die like an endangered species starved of its basic nutrients." Gottman cites a "magic ratio" of five positive interactions to every negative one. I adopted this concept for our marriage, which has helped me both contain negative words and try to consciously create loving moments to maintain that positive balance.

We needed to give our marriage attention and intention, to intentionally dedicate time to nurturing our relationship. Sometimes, when work erupts, when children need our singular focus, when other urgent demands steal our attention, we assume that the marriage can wait. The marriage often becomes our lowest priority when it needs to be our first. We are juggling all these balls, trying to keep each one in the air. What we forget is that some of them are rubber balls and some of them are glass. If we drop certain balls, like the soccer snack, the PTA altogether, the professional dinner, or even our religious services, they will bounce back. We will survive. But some of the balls are glass, and if we drop those ones, like our daughter's school play, our son's broken arm, each other's need to talk and be heard, or—God forbid—our anniversary, it may be more difficult for us to pick up the pieces.

We learned to take time to consciously set our priorities. On my office and cell phones, my speed dial reflected my priorities. Number 1 was always Matt, then came home, childcare, school, and extended family. Of course, on any given day, I might take the call or not depending on the context, but the overarching priority was always clear.

We had committed to our anniversary dinners, which eventually grew into anniversary weekends away. We enjoyed wonderful family vacations but also took time away without the kids, another benefit of our nearby extended family. It surprised and delighted us how quickly we could drop back into a deep emotional connection if we could just get out of the house and away from the constant call of family logistics. We realized that these times away were vital to the health of our marriage—nurturing for us and essential for our children. We often encouraged other couples who were reluctant to take time away that the best thing they could do for their kids was to invest in their marriage.

At the end of our difficult seventh year, Matt and I took our anniversary weekend away to the Northern California coastal town of Mendocino. The town is romantic and quaint, set atop broad seascapes. We had reservations at the Little Albion River Inn, overlooking the rugged coast. It was a long drive up the winding coastal highway, but our arrival was perfectly timed for sunset over the ocean. We settled in, took a walk along the ocean bluff, and then prepared for dinner.

Once we had ordered our dinner and wine, we began to consider the past year. It had threatened our marriage more than any other. Scenes from the past several months came into focus. The epic hug and near infidelity he had entertained came back to me. It had happened while I worked, sat with my sister and her son in the hospital, expending myself beyond my capacity as the circumstances demanded.

"Oh!" I remembered. "You were terrible to me!"

I had pushed away all that emotion during the year in order to keep up with my responsibilities, and it now rose from my heart to my throat. Matt portrayed it as a classic seven-year itch, trying to minimize the real risk to our marriage and family. But, to me, it had been seriously threatening, leaving me with a devastating sense of fragility in our marriage. I felt terribly hurt, betrayed, and angry, all of which came literally pouring forth over dinner. I cried through most of the lavish meal, as we talked it all through again, expressing some of the emotion that I hadn't been able to indulge at the time.

The expensive food was tasteless in my mouth as we kept up the façade of our romantic dinner while delving into the depths of our marriage. The waiter would approach and seeing the intensity and tears, retreat again. In retrospect, we were able to recognize the distance that had grown between us during the year, my emotional unavailability to him and the family with my work and commute, and his recourse to another source of affection. Over dinner, we rehashed each of our hurt feelings and acknowledged the temptation of finding solace elsewhere. By the time dessert arrived, we had turned the page. That chapter had closed; we were ready to move on—together.

I was glad to be in a faraway place where no one would recognize me, although the next day, as we walked through shops in the small town, I had more than one person say, "Weren't you at the Little River Inn last night?"

"Yes," I said and smiled, thinking, *Yes, I was the one blubbering all through my dinner!* But I didn't really care. We had done the work that we needed to do that night to remember, repair, and resolve. We'd gotten our story straight and come to a mutual understanding of a most difficult year.

Balance is not static; it is a dynamic process of constant adjustment. During those early years after we returned to California, we were both committed to developing careers and managing the demands of a busy household, and that balance often eluded us. With my commute to San Francisco and a full-time law practice, I had very little time with my family. I didn't see the children before leaving for the train each morning and had only an hour or so with them in the evenings. I was unable to attend teacher conferences or doctor appointments during the day. I was also spending occasional evenings and weekends with my sister and her son.

Sometimes, someone needs to draw a picture to get your attention. A year later, during an evening open house at our daughter's nursery school, the parents roamed the room full of children's artwork. The children had each drawn a picture of their families. I was happy to find Cassedy's drawing on the bulletin board, but on closer examination, it broke my heart. Stick figure Cassedy was holding hands with Daddy on one side and Tyler on the other, with a circle drawn around the three of them. Stick figure Mommy stood outside the circle. Struck with sadness, I wanted to dismiss it. But a week later, Tyler made a very similar drawing and I realized my life had gotten way out of balance. Ironically, I had become that unavailable, work-focused partner I had not wanted to marry. I needed more time with my family, and I knew that time could be limited. My sister had just lost her only son at age 11. There were no guarantees that my children would be there when I decided I had time for them.

I was working on a family law case and was surprised when the opposing attorney invited me to visit their Palo Alto office and consider joining their firm. Not seriously thinking about a move, I strolled through the offices, keeping up a polite conversation. When I looked out from their floor to ceiling conference room window across the small town, the proximity to my home was striking. I could almost actually see my house from there. To dispense with the daily commute to San Francisco would gain me 12 or more hours a week with my family. I would be near enough to get away for children's midday conferences, performances, games, or emergencies. This was a critical opportunity to reestablish the balance in our family life and create a more sustainable work commitment for me. Matt and I talked about it and agreed it was the right move for us. Although it might have meant less income in the long run, we recognized that the money wasn't worth the price of our presence to the family. Time—more than money—became an ongoing priority for us.

Relocating my work close to home opened up tremendous space in the days. I had mornings to jog on my own or with Matt. I could have breakfast with the kids and help get them off to school before my 10-minute drive to the office. At the end of the day, I could pick up the kids or even bring them to the office for a homework session while I finished a few things. Although not much homework or legal work was accomplished during those visits, the children became familiar with the office and the people I worked with. We settled into a more balanced flow between work and home, between Matt's work, my work, and our shared family activities. We decided to have a third child and welcomed our son Timmy, almost 10 years younger than Tyler and 5 years younger than Cassedy.

We finally implemented my college dream of both working and sharing responsibility at home. We each worked four days a week. Matt took Thursdays at home, and I had Fridays. The children needed childcare for just three days a week, and we were grateful to have my mom spend those three afternoons with them. We each committed a weekday to home and parenting. I spent many Friday mornings in the children's classrooms and drove on school field trips. When the children no longer needed my time, I kept Fridays for myself. The four-day workweek gave each of us dedicated time for the family, as well as precious time for our individual pursuits.

> *It is not only the threat of conflict and active disagreement that can undermine a marriage. It can also be the inconspicuous, infectious, insidiously slow drift of separate work, separate friends, separate interests until the separate exceeds the joint and the road back together seems harder than the road apart.*

Practice

The everyday is as blessed as we make it. A spiritual practice is an intentional act that we do on a regular, repetitious basis. With commitment and reverence, we trust that the practice will improve our mental, emotional, and spiritual health. Kissing could be adopted as a spiritual practice, to cultivate our own happiness and to foster connection with our partner.

Make kissing a spiritual practice. Kiss good morning. Kiss goodbye at leaving and hello upon returning. Kiss good night—always, every day, four times a day.

There are good reasons we kiss. Kissing sets off a chemical reaction in our brains that releases hormones that make us feel that giddy sense of being in love. We also have more nerve endings in our lips than in most other parts of our bodies. When two sets of lips come together, it just feels good. It also gets better with age. Researchers have found that kissing frequency is correlated to relationship satisfaction and that kissing is generally more important in long-term relationships, particularly for women.

Over time, our marital kisses might become perfunctory, even unconscious. It may seem meaningless, and perhaps, some of the time, it is. But seen as a practice, a habit of the heart, even when seemingly perfunctory, each kiss contributes to the overall practice. And the practice holds the promise of the occasional kiss that sparks, that transcends the ordinary. Just like blessing ourselves, saying a grace before meals, a morning meditation, or a bedtime prayer ritual, it may often seem rote, even unconscious. But then there will be a moment when something breaks through our routine. The cumulation of intention is rewarded with an unexpected depth of feeling. We can infuse the daily practice of marriage with affection, attention, and our best intentions.

Reflection

- Is our relationship more prone to conflict or to drift? What could I do to lower the temperature on conflict or raise the temperature on connection? (This is not to suggest that all conflict is negative. Some conflict is to be expected and it is how we manage our conflicts that is important. In fact, avoidance of conflict can lead directly to drift.)
- Do we make it a priority to spend time together away from the home and family? One young couple recently referred to it as an "off-site."

- What keeps us from taking time for ourselves? How might we overcome these obstacles?
- If I were to keep a tally, how would our positive interactions compare to our negative interactions? Do we meet Gottman's magic ratio of 5:1?
- What are some creative positive interactions I might cultivate (flowers, messages, extra help with household jobs, humor, kissing)?

Resources

Gottman, John, *Why Marriages Succeed or Fail, and How You Can Make Sure Yours Last*, p. 64, Simon & Schuster (1994).

Benson, Kyle, "The Magic Relationship Ratio, According to Science." https://www.gottman.com/blog/the-magic-relationship-ratio-according-science

Santos-Longhurst, Adrienne, "Why Do We Kiss" https://www.healthline.com/health/why-do-we-kiss

Wlodarski, R., Dunbar, R.I.M. "Examining the Possible Functions of Kissing in Romantic Relationships," https://doi.org/10.1007/s10508-013-0190-1

7

THE MARRIAGE STORY

Friday night

Both Matt and I were relieved to settle in after a typically busy week and the atypical new complication of his secret admirer. Matt had spent all day at a professional seminar—on infidelity of all things—but didn't want to talk about it. I smiled at the irony but sensed he was hoping to gain a footing as the ground shifted beneath him. I knew we would have time to talk during the weekend and was fine to leave it for the evening.

With both Cassedy and Timmy staying over with friends for the night, we relaxed with a movie after dinner. In *The Story of Us*, Bruce Willis and Michelle Pfeiffer play a couple who are separating. They plan to tell their children when the kids return from camp at the end of the summer. A bit of a busman's holiday for us, the movie replays their many arguments and various attempts at counseling. Although this couple never seems to gain much insight into their conflict, they continue to look back on their marriage with tenderness and a sense of destiny. Watching it, I felt sad but also comforted by their story, which seemed to carry them through.

We can gain much wisdom and healing by sharing stories. Our societal rituals for doing so have largely fallen away, but when it happens, there is no mistaking the value of simply recognizing ourselves in the story and knowing that we are not alone.

Our marriage story began unexpectedly. As we graduated from college, both Matt and I intended to continue our studies. Neither of us had solidified a plan beyond taking a year off to work, save some money, and sort it out. As we each completed applications for graduate programs and prioritized our separate plans for the future, our relationship was relegated to uncertainty. Letters of acceptance or rejection began to arrive, and our choices were narrowed. Matt was applying to medical schools, a daunting task at the time, and had only a couple of possibilities. Once all of Matt's results were in, he had not been accepted to medical school, which upended his long-held dream. Dejected, he decided to stay in California, work for another year, and apply to psychology graduate programs instead. In the meantime, I had applied to a handful of law schools, a couple on the West Coast and a couple on the East Coast. This set up my ultimate decision of whether to stay close to home and Matt or to head 3,000 miles across the country.

I loved Matt and wanted our relationship to continue. Not one to rely on my feelings, I reasoned through the benefits of our relationship. We were compatible, and we also challenged each other intellectually, physically, sexually, spiritually. I wanted a partner who would inspire me and embrace our growth over time. Most importantly, Matt had demonstrated that he could support me and my goals. In fact, his confidence in me often exceeded my own and inspired me to go further. He was adventurous and athletic, drawing me into activities beyond my comfort zone. One day early in our courtship, he suited me up in scuba gear and took me diving in Monterey Bay. He opened an entirely new world in the iridescent rainbows of the kelp forest.

As the time neared for me to make a decision, we went backpacking to Jasper National Park in Canada; this was something else I wouldn't have ventured on my own. I pondered as we hiked up the rocky trail alongside the descending stream. I knew that Matt was not ready to make a long-term commitment. He had only had one other serious girlfriend, while I had been in a steady stream of relationships since I was 14. He needed time and space to sort out his life plan, which had just taken an unexpected left turn. I realized I needed to give him some distance. I needed to trust that life would sort itself out. I decided to start law school at Georgetown University, in Washington, DC, that fall.

Our parting was ambivalent, at least for me. As much as I wanted to go and knew that was best for both of us, I didn't want to close the door on our relationship. Along that rocky trail, I negotiated mightily for an open-door break up, not even sure what that meant. Granted, we were going our separate ways—no strings attached, each of us free to explore—but also without closing the door on reconnecting if that was something we both wanted in the future. Maybe I just wasn't willing to let go, to leave with a broken heart. It seemed easier to leave with an open heart, and I was sincerely open for both myself and Matt, although I secretly believed that, with a little distance (or a lot), he would come to appreciate me even more. So I left.

That fall semester in DC was exciting. I met people from all around the country. I shared a house with three other people and became familiar with the Metro system, my route to the law school, and a few other detours. I was thrilled to be learning the law and living in what seemed to be the center of law and politics, with the US Supreme Court, Capitol Hill, and the White House surrounding the law school. Happy to be on my own and not in a relationship for the first time, I was surprised when a new friendship with one of my classmates quickly turned to flirtation and then a light romance. I set limits on this new relationship; I was still hoping that Matt and I might reconnect.

Meanwhile, Matt and I wrote letters back and forth occasionally, casually. Then we began to talk on the phone, careful not to pry. At that time, long distance phone calls were expensive. The rates were lower if I called him after 11:00 p.m., which was only 8:00 p.m. for him in California. It became more and more difficult to hang up, and our calls went on sometimes for hours. We were each thriving, but there was a longing that came through the telephone line. As the fall semester was winding down and I was busy studying for final exams, I received a letter from Matt with an invitation to come "home" for Christmas, to stay with him during my winter break. As much as I had enjoyed my freedom and adventure, the invitation warmed my open heart. I was excited for our reunion.

I arrived in California late in the evening a few days before Christmas. Matt was working the night shift at his nursing assistant job at the Veteran's Hospital. I made myself at home in the room we had shared before I left. It was nice to have a chance to settle into the familiar space on my own and to sleep. I awoke to Matt's return and a sweet reunion. As we held each other again, I felt a strong sense of belonging, of home. We spent two luxurious weeks together, including holiday time with both of our families and a ski trip to Lake Tahoe, all while talking, sharing, making love, and weaving dreams together. Matt had applied to several psychology programs in the DC area to begin the next fall. Maybe we would live together in DC. A future was unfolding.

Then it was time for me to go. I returned to Washington in early January with a new commitment to Matt. Like me, Matt had had a relationship during our time apart, and like me, he had broken it off before our Christmas reunion. We had decided to spend the summer together in California and for him to join me in DC the next fall.

I settled into a productive rhythm at school. I had done well on my first semester exams and dove back into my studies. A couple weeks later, it occurred to me that my period was late. I was tempted to dismiss it with the travel and the change of routine, but I realized that I could be pregnant. I had gone off the pill when I had left California in the fall, and we had been using a less effective birth control method over the holidays. Normally, I would have been worried and anxious, but I wasn't afraid or upset. I felt a calm commitment to wait and see, to simply hold the possibility. A few days later, my intuition was confirmed with a positive pregnancy test. The first thing I wanted to do was call Matt. This was ours to process together. Without giving it more thought, I called him.

"Hullo?" he mumbled, clearly waking from a dead sleep. Although it was late morning in DC, it was early in California, and he had worked a late-night shift at the hospital.

"Well, did you mean what you said over Christmas?" I hinted.

"Huh?" he said, still getting his bearings.

"About our future together?" I asked. Met with silence—and, I supposed, confusion—I just told him. "I'm pregnant."

The silence persisted, but I could sense the fog clearing and the picture coming into view.

"What? Oh. Wow."

Even though I had had a few days with this possibility in the back of my mind, I had not fully digested the reality myself. We had talked hypothetically before about unplanned pregnancy and what we would do. Although we had disagreed religiously and politically about choice and the right to life, we had agreed that we—at that time in our lives, with all the resources we had available to us—could not, in good conscience, terminate a healthy pregnancy, however inconvenient. But how we would navigate the reality of a shared child with our relationship and each of our futures was uncertain.

I don't recall a lot of words being spoken as we took the news in together. The question was whether we would accept this impetus to begin a life together. In that early morning phone call, we decided. The answer was yes. We would embrace the promise of marriage and parenthood. My heart was already deeply embedded in this tiny being, my own embodiment of our promise. We agreed to talk more in the evening and hung up, transformed. The future was suddenly taking the shape of a new life.

We spoke further that evening and began laying the foundation for our new life. We decided to get married during my spring break in a few months, in California. We announced to everyone that we were getting married and having a baby. There was no secret and no shame. Our wedding invitation featured a single rose with a small bud, drawing on the wisdom from *The Little Prince*: "You become responsible, forever, for what you have tamed. You are responsible for your rose." We felt blessed and called into marriage by this baby, and we stepped wholeheartedly into that blessing.

We planned the wedding in those short couple of months, with loving support from our families and friends. Matt's sister printed our invitations. My dress was made by a friend of the family, complete with pearl embroidery and every flounce and detail I could imagine. While I bristled at the patriarchal tradition of a diamond ring as a vestige of the husband's proprietary rights over the bride, I had been gifted with a family diamond from my great aunt. Setting this diamond for my wedding ring solved my political dilemma and still allowed me my girl's best friend. We carefully planned the readings and music for the wedding ceremony, which was held at a small Catholic church. It was officiated by Matt's brother, a Catholic priest, followed by an outdoor reception at Matt's parents' home. It was simple, meaningful, perfect. We took in the good wishes of those gathered and let our love and confidence in our future shine. We were no different from so many young couples celebrating a wedding with no idea of all that is to come. We felt that, so long as we had each other, we were prepared to move into the unknown future.

How we crafted our story out of our circumstances was critical to the foundation of our marriage. I had woven a story leading up to that point, but this new reality—this new life—demanded to be written into the script. Crisis truly can be opportunity—an invitation, however abrupt. We welcomed the pregnancy as a blessing, not an accident. We named our son Matthew Tyler, Matthew meaning "gift from God." Together, we crossed the threshold into our commitment and new life. If either of us had felt otherwise, the story would have been quite different.

The marriage story isn't happening to us; we are creating it as we go. There is the external choice of what to do and the internal choice of how to give it meaning, how to hold the experience, and how to view yourself and your partner in your life's unfolding events. Maybe the most important part of sharing of our marriage story is what we tell ourselves and our partners. People who live together—sharing a home, a family, a bed—can too often be living different, even incompatible stories. They keep these stories bottled up to separately ruminate over on sleepless nights. Creating a shared narrative can be essential to mutual understanding—and often to healing. If we share our stories, we will see where story lines don't match up and the incompatible plot points. We can reconfigure the narrative to reconcile the diverging points of view, synthesizing a new truth that both of us can live with and grow from.

This was one benefit of our anniversary year-in-review ritual. We got our stories straight, synched up our narrative. On our third anniversary, we took our first real vacation to Jamaica between my DC and California bar exams. We spent our tenth on the coast in Santa Cruz with three-week-old Timmy. On our 16th, we traveled to Kauai and visited the famous Fern Grotto, serenaded by the Hawaiian Wedding Song. But we also had some difficult years. As I have shared, our second anniversary dinner was ugly, and our seventh was equally rough. We not only got away for relaxation together but also took time to reflect on our lives, our dreams and lived logistics, and to align our view, both out the rear-view mirror and the windshield ahead.

Matt and I both chose to work in the divorce business. I gravitated to family law while Matt was still finishing his doctorate. He followed me and developed an expertise in working with coparents after separation. We have seen the damage that people do to one another and their children in separation and divorce.

I listened day after day to the stories of the spouse, my client, who never saw it coming—of the "model" marriages decimated by conflict, isolation, infidelity, and separation. Clients arrived in my office still in a state of shock as they insisted that theirs had been the perfect marriage. *Ask anyone*, they would plead. My clients' stories reminded me daily of the hazards.

I have seen how the story of the marriage gets rewritten at the time of separation and divorce. It begins with the decision to end the marriage. In the case of infidelity and betrayal, the story is quickly reconstructed: "He is not the person I married," or "What else has she been hiding?"

The aggrieved partner feels duped, misled. Only now do they see clearly. There is a dissonance between years of a seemingly happy marriage and the discovery of an affair. The deception calls into question all of the trust in the marriage that has gone before. It rocks the marriage to the core. In the face of this betrayal, the earlier belief in the partner must be false; the story must be a lie. In this way, marriages of many years are rewritten as though all of those years were unhappy. The cheating partner, the story must go, has been hiding their true self—and their infidelity.

Infidelity is not the only path to a marriage's end. Maybe the couple grew apart, shifting values or priorities creating incompatibility. Still, there is a sense that, if the marriage cannot last and the vows are not kept, the entire marriage is a failure. The story must be reconstructed to cast this shadow across time. Perhaps this is the truth, but perhaps it is just a way of coping with the shame or sadness that the marriage is ending.

I encouraged my clients to embrace their happy memories and to remember the good years, even as they made a decision to separate. We might allow a narrative of a healthy marriage that has simply run its course. Genuine happy and healthy years may have simply shifted to become unhappy for one or both partners. Perhaps the final work of the marriage is to give it an honest review, to celebrate its joys and successes. It may be time to take responsibility for our own part in its pain and shortcomings, to learn the lessons, and to extract wisdom from the experience.

Maybe it helped our marriage to spend hours each day listening to couples literally dissolve their marriages, to deconstruct the romance and reconstruct the story of their lives to fit with the sorry end. But being immersed in divorce could also have created a toxic emotional environment of fear and insecurity. Good or bad, that is the irony of our marriage: We live and breathe divorce while working to create and preserve a healthy marriage.

During our difficult midlife passage, we attended a day-long workshop for couples entitled "Conflict in Marriage." Freeing up a Saturday for both of us was a challenge. But it seemed like just what we needed as we struggled with our disparate goals and difficult communication. The day was rich, full of heartfelt conversations, games, laughter, and wisdom. One of the exercises involved couples choosing a fortune cookie with two fortunes, one for each partner, with two perspectives on a common conflict, such as:

> *You never bring me flowers anymore/You never fix yourself up anymore;* or
> *You don't respond to my advances/You are only affectionate when you want to have sex.*

First of all, who knew there were "common conflicts"—that every other couple is having the same argument on a weekly, monthly, or yearly basis? We certainly didn't.

A couple would choose a cookie and then each act out the respective sides of the conflict, to the hysterical laughter of the rest of us. This laughter was borne of full identification with the issue. We heard that we were not alone, that behind the veil of these other marriages, there was struggle and conflict. It diffused the heat of our personal arguments to see that they arose out of age-old tensions, which are almost inevitable in a long-term marriage.

As helpful and comforting as this was, what struck me about the workshop was that, although it was quite well attended and excellently presented, there was no one there we knew. When we arrived, a woman came over, graciously welcomed us, and asked where we taught marriage preparation. We looked at each other, confused, and admitted that we weren't teaching; we were just there to attend the workshop. As the day went on, we realized that, of about 200 people, we were one of only a few couples who were there on our own account, not as teachers or ministers, but just as a married couple. The workshop was not only preaching to the choir; it was preaching to the preachers! We were puzzled why more couples hadn't come and felt sorry they had missed it.

When Matt and I talked about it later, we realized that perhaps to show up for a workshop on marital conflict was an admission that you were struggling, which was not something most couples wanted to admit. It also seemed that this helpful instruction was reserved for couples before the wedding, when they would have little experience or interest in marital tensions. This information was vital support for couples in the middle of their marriage.

In my work as a divorce lawyer, I felt sad for the marriages that, in my view, could have survived and even thrived if they had received support at crucial times in their relationship. Something like this workshop—sharing the normal struggles of marriage and ways of working through them together—could be so helpful. There were plenty of marriage books out there, some more helpful than others. There were also ample other resources for couples, including workshops, videos, and retreats. But, like the program we had attended, it seemed that people were reluctant to access them. Like me on our second anniversary, struggling couples were terrified that if they admitted there was a problem, the marriage was doomed. This is an unfortunate side effect of a culture that subscribes to the "happily ever after" myth. It creates a barrier for married couples to access resources that could assist them or support their very real marriage.

Marriage work is hard to do alone, especially in the throes of conflict.

More than premarital education, married couples need ongoing support to navigate the challenges of married life. This can begin at the wedding, with the witnesses and officiant committing to continue to be present to support the couple. It can expand to other couples, who may live near each other, know each other through work, attend childbirth or parenting programs together, or meet in a child's school or sports program. Time with friends, such as boys' or girls' nights out, offer a chance to blow off steam and also to gain perspective within a safe community of friends. In the best case, those friends respect and support the marriage while providing a place to complain, fume, question, and maybe even laugh. It takes a risk to reach out, but many young couples are hungry for that connection.

At the end of the summer following my first year of law school, when I was eight months pregnant with Tyler, Matt and I drove from California across the country to DC. The moving truck was loaded with our third-hand furnishings and still-boxed wedding gifts. Matt did the heavy lifting into our graduate student apartment; I was exhausted from the last leg of our drive, and my ankles had swollen into melons. Despite the fatigue, we both felt excited to begin this next chapter together.

That weekend, we met other new graduate students at a Labor Day brunch in our apartment courtyard. I immediately connected with Mary, a young engineering student in the next building, who was newly married and had just arrived from Chicago. A couple weeks later, as I sat nursing my newborn son, Mary knocked on my door to see if the baby had arrived. We had our first conversation, three hours of sharing about both of our recent weddings, our husbands, families, and graduate studies. That was the beginning of a lifelong friendship. Matt and I formed a chosen extended family with Mary and her husband, Mike, during our years in graduate housing. We shared meals, childcare, weekend outings, and lots of conversation.

After four years together, Mary and Mike told us they would be moving away for a new job. We were surprised and tried to be upbeat, but then I burst into tears. We all cried together, acknowledging the importance of our friendship and mutual support. Then we made a promise; we committed to seeing each other every year, one way or another. All the years since, we have gotten together, visiting each other's homes or meeting up for joint family vacations. Our three children and their four have become chosen family, as we each became godparents to one of the other's daughters. In our experience, it is a rare friendship where all four people in the couples, as well as the children, get along. Thankfully, we were wise enough to understand how precious our connection was and to commit to nurturing it over time. We lifted our veils and shared intimately with these friends through many joys and sorrows.

We found additional support for our marriage in a couple's group that we joined through our church community shortly after our return to California. The priest invited five young married couples to meet with him once a month for a potluck evening in the home of one of the couples. The monthly meeting had a structure and a purpose to support each marriage through conversation and shared prayer. We began the meeting with a "whip around"—sharing about our prior month over dinner. We then had time for prayer, reflection, and discussion led by one of the couples. We closed each evening with a prayer and a song.

Each couple also made certain commitments to the group,

including finding time once a month for each couple to discuss their marriage with one another. Our young marriages were laden with responsibilities. All of us had children, and most of us had two careers. There was little time for a reflective conversation. For many of us, the conversation took place in the car en route to the meeting. But at least once a month, even if for 20 minutes in the car, we talked about our marriage—about our connection and the pressures of work and family—and we recommitted to making it better the next month. We studied, we shared, and we listened. We wrote our marriage story together.

Matt and I found our place in this community of marriages—some stronger than ours, some faltering. We joined a community of marathoners, each of us members with our own vulnerabilities and ambitions. We shared tips on getting through, on training and joys of the race. And we kept going, one foot in front of the other, for the duration. Our group continued meeting together for over 20 years, including during this midlife disconnect.

My divorce work has led me to write, teach, and minister to married couples to provide some of the insight and support that seems so sorely missing in our culture of almost disposable marriage. My marriage work also informs my divorce work. I have found my work with divorcing couples challenging, gratifying, and always interesting. I have been honored and humbled to be admitted behind the veil into the internal workings of marriage as clients share their journey, the triumphs and tragedies, and the breaking points that have led them to my office. As I work to sort out the legal and financial issues, to educate my clients about the law and their options, I also try to provide perspective and support. I see my role as advocate and advisor in the legal process, as well as a guide through this significant life transition. I shepherd people through the dissolution and finding new ground.

Matt and I reflect frequently on our own marriage as we swim in the deep waters of marital discord. Our marriage is far from perfect. We struggled through many changes and events in our early years, navigating conflict and somehow managing to find ways to engage with each other and sort through our differences. We have learned the importance of staying connected and keeping our relationship fresh even in the daily routines of family life. We are vigilant about not only preserving but enriching our marriage, taking time away from work and kids to nurture our intimacy. We have actively sought opportunities to share openly with other couples about the challenges of marriage.

Marriage, like life, is full of drama. It is full of stories building and resolving and a new story taking hold, building to climax, and crashing on the shore to rebuild again. It is the ordinary drama of everyday life, of every moment. It is the drama of contentment and change. It requires a steady hand on the tiller and constant adjustment to remain on course. Outwardly, it may appear dull, but internally, it is wildly dynamic, in constant motion.

> ***The marriage story isn't happening to us;***
> ***we are creating it as we go.***

Reflection

What is the real story of a marriage? What is the climax? How is it resolved? Yes, the story of marriage has a climax—several, multiple climaxes. It is a roller coaster of constant ups and downs, twists and turns. This is ironic, since, culturally, we cast it as static—a straight line of happily ever after.

- What is the story I tell myself about our marriage? Do we share the story?
- Is the story true? Does it need Refreshment? Revision? Remembrance?
- How does our story make me feel?
- What are the primary supports for our marriage?
- Where can we turn for encouragement and perspective in times of difficulty?

Resources

Finding peer support for your marriage can be critical to surviving difficult times. Seek out couples' groups and supports in your community and religious organizations. You may have to create your own supportive group of couples, especially for same-sex or nontraditional marriages. Even gatherings not explicitly focused on marriage but organized around children or other life events can provide essential companionship and support, such as childbirth classes, childcare, school, sports, or church activities. Predictable times of stress or transition present opportunities for mutual support.

Whatever you may think about the Catholic Church, and

I have my own ambivalence, it is one of the best resources for ongoing marriage support. For marriage support opportunities through the Catholic community, visit For Your Marriage at https://www.foryourmarriage.org.

Teams of Our Lady, or Equipes Notre-Dame, is an international lay movement begun by four couples seeking the help of their priest, Fr. Henri Caffarel, in 1939. The organization supports married couples by creating a community of faith among groups of couples. Joined by a priest, the group commits to gathering, sharing, and supporting one another in their marriage and seeking Christ together. There is a prayerful and spiritual focus to their work by following specific practices called the Endeavors and monthly meetings that consist of a shared meal, prayer, and deep sharing about the realities of married life. Teams of Our Lady has active groups throughout the United States and over 90 other countries; for more information see https://www.teamsofourlady.org.

Same-sex and other LGBTQ+ relationships could connect with the local LGBTQ+ Community Center for support: https://www.lgbtcenters.org.

8

SECRETS AND DECEIT

Saturday morning

Matt and I decided to take advantage of the kids still being at their sleepovers and headed out for a long jog along the nearby Baylands trail. The flat dirt path winding through the marshlands of the San Francisco Bay, rich with birdlife, gave us the opportunity to talk and get some exercise at the same time. In his runner's breath, Matt told me about his seminar on infidelity from the day before.

"What destroys a marriage is not so much the act of infidelity but the deceit, the breach of trust," he reported as we trotted along.

That made sense to me. No one wants to be played for a fool, trusting and believing in something false—especially when it comes to opening our hearts and making ourselves vulnerable.

"Deceit undermines the marriage, even without infidelity. If you don't trust your partner, the same kinds of insecurities and defenses kick in." He paused and added, "But it seems to me that couples should be able to have some secrets, some private parts of themselves. You don't have to share everything." He took another few breaths. "It was crazy to have this workshop in the middle of this woman's messages."

He was clearly troubled by his secret admirer, the conflicting pulls of his desire and fidelity, temptation and guilt. I listened, curious how he was feeling about all of this. At the end of the workshop, what had Matt learned? Where did he see himself in these couples' stories, in the therapist's postmortem?

"You don't seem too concerned about this secret admirer," he said, a note of accusation in his voice. "You're not telling me anything about what I should do."

Surprised to be put on the spot, I stammered, "What's to do? You haven't heard from her again, have you?"

"No," he lied.

"Then there's nothing to do." I shrugged and kept jogging, relieved to be off the hot seat.

Of course, I was ruminating on the secret admirer and Matt's reactions. It seemed he was looking for my support in handling his torturous ambivalence, to set the limits that he was struggling with for himself. Even though we both knew that deceit was dangerous in a marriage, Matt and I had different thresholds for self-disclosure. Matt had always had more of an inclination toward secrets. I tended to process my feelings through conversation and was more comfortable with sharing. But I had a few of my own secrets as well. He had openly shared the messages from the secret admirer, but I was not being honest with him about their origin. My secret—that may have been getting out of hand—was making me increasingly anxious.

Jogging along that afternoon just a week before, I felt mired in my inability to engage Matt in a meaningful conversation about our midlife disconnect. I was burdened by the prospect of years of marital therapy, and the spark of somehow starting afresh caught hold of my imagination. When I arrived back home, Matt had suggested that fantasy and play might be necessary in a marriage—in our marriage. Although I had rejected the suggestion, it started working on my psyche. The next morning, driving to work, on a whim, I had called Matt's office phone and left that silly secret admirer voicemail. I felt so foolish. I was sure he would recognize my voice; I hadn't even disguised it. But he didn't! So, I took a chance by putting the note in his car, of course disguising the handwriting.

His paranoid reaction and sincere distress surprised me. What had started as a playful fantasy seemed to be more troubling than titillating for Matt. Although Matt was comfortable with his sexuality, an aspect of his masculine desire tangled up with shame and humiliation was being triggered. I didn't want to just abandon the masquerade, but I realized I needed to relieve him of this anxiety. I needed to move the game to revelation and hopefully connection sooner rather than later.

I decided to bring the flirtation to a head, a face-to-face meeting. But how? I couldn't risk another call or even a note. Email would be perfect, but, of course, he would recognize my address. Despite my limited tech skills, I was able to set up another email address under our shared account. Using the address "Sameri," a not so clever play on secret admirer, I composed an email inviting him to meet me for drinks that Sunday, piña coladas no less, with a blatant reference to the old song. I hit "send," feeling silly and excited all at once. That was Friday morning.

That same day, I had coffee with my good friend and couldn't help but let her in on the secret. When I told her I was having an affair, she almost spit out her coffee. I assured her not to worry; the affair was with Matt. She gave me a troubled and questioning scowl, so I backed up and filled her in, up to my invitation to meet up at the bar and the big anticipated reveal. She knew both Matt and me well, and I respected her advice, so I was surprised when she gave me an ominous warning.

"This is not a good idea. This could totally blow up in your face."

"How?" I asked, disappointed and confused.

"What if he gets angry?" she asked. "What if he feels like you are setting him up? Like this was a test or a trap?"

She continued with her warning that I should be very careful, and I began to question the whole crazy scheme. It was not a test. I was prepared to accept Matt's response, whether he shared the messages with me or not. The object was to engage him in a game, a fantasy, not to catch him in a trap. But how would he see it? Would it backfire?

He hadn't shown me the email from Sameri, which, of course, I knew he had received the day before. I could hardly be upset with him, since I was deceiving him with the whole charade. This game suddenly felt much more dangerous.

From my experience with divorce, I knew the devastating impact of real affairs. The couples were blindsided by the tornado of the affair, powerful, seemingly coming out of nowhere, tearing up the ground, tossing their well-constructed home into the air and hurling it, swirling it, and, then, just as quickly vanishing. The house crashes to Earth and deconstructs into rubble, never to be put together again. Casting blame between the couple will ensure that any possibility of new construction will be pulled back into the rubble.

I knew that the pulls toward infidelity were many and complex. It was difficult to sort through all of the factors that may have contributed to it. The dynamics of relationships included the conscious and unconscious motives of both partners. While some affairs were conscious choices, many were unconscious impulses, working beneath the surface and then erupting into awareness at moments of vulnerability. Whatever the impetus of the affair, the efforts to recover from infidelity were mired in the issues that preceded it, as well as the anger and betrayal, the blame and shame arising in its aftermath.

I worked with one couple in mediation, meeting with them together without their lawyers. They were an older couple, in their late 60s, at the end of a long-term marriage. When we first met, the husband told me their story. They had a good traditional marriage. He worked hard all day to support the family while his wife kept the home and cared for the children. Now, their children were grown and on their own, he was nearing retirement, and they were entering their golden years, with time and money to spend together. One day a few months before, he had come home unannounced in the middle of the day and interrupted his wife and her lover in flagrante delicto. He was outraged and confused. In the aftermath, the wife confessed that she had been seeing this other man over the past 10 years. The husband was devastated and unable to fathom this level of deceit and betrayal over such a long period. After he recounted the story, they told me they loved each other, and they both wanted to put this breach behind them and continue their marriage together.

It was a powerful story, and I carried it with me as I went home that evening. Although the story was quite dramatic, I was impressed that they sincerely wanted to move beyond the affair and heal the marriage. The next time I met with them, I was hopeful we could begin to sort things through a bit and that maybe I would hear more from the wife's perspective.

As we began our next session, the husband again took the floor to retell the terrible story of his wife's infidelity, repeating the details to her and to me, although we both knew quite well the sequence of events. I tried with various questions and suggestions to move the discussion forward, but he was not ready to let go of the story, and she remained silent. We ended again with their mutual desire to put the affair behind them and move on but with no real progress in shifting the conversation in that direction.

At our third meeting, when he again recited the story of her affair, the wife did finally speak up. She apologized to him again and sincerely. She repeated her desire to stay together and to move forward. But, she said, she did not believe he could ever let go of the story. And she was unwilling to continue to allow him to beat her up with the litany of her transgressions. He was surprised, defensive, and self-righteous. He felt entitled to his outrage and was, sadly, unwilling to move beyond it. Interestingly, we never talked about the wife's feelings about the affair, her understanding of her motivations, and what she got out of the relationship. Perhaps aspects of herself that had been suppressed in the marriage were given life in the illicit relationship. Even as they talked about the affair, he was not willing to hear her.

Ultimately, they were unable to get past the affair, and we began work on the terms of their separation and divorce. What has stayed with me all these years was the tremendous sadness they both felt in losing the marriage despite their sincere desire to stay together. It seemed the affair held more power over their psyches than they could resolve. The infidelity was devastating, but the 10-year deceit was unrecoverable.

I saw firsthand the devastating consequences of deceit. I consulted with another woman whose marriage was shattered in a mind-bending series of discoveries. First, she found out that her husband of two years was having an affair even as they struggled to become pregnant. Then, she realized that he had emptied their joint bank account and run up several credit cards in her name to the limit. He had not been working as she believed for several months and had failed to keep up their mortgage payments. Finally, he was gone, disappeared without a trace. Not only was her heart broken, but to make matters worse, she was also bankrupt. Because he could not be located, she was left holding the empty financial bag and had to file for bankruptcy on top of divorce. Everything she had come to believe about who her husband was—what their marriage was—turned out to be a lie. It was devastating, not only financially but personally, as she tried to fathom how she could have been so deceived.

Emotional or psychological affairs, where the couple never engages in sexual conduct and may never even meet in person, can be as powerful a betrayal as physical infidelity. Deceiving a spouse about other issues can also undermine the foundation of trust in the marriage—habits such as drinking, smoking, or gambling that continue covertly despite promises to quit. A partner might hold a secret about family history or children from the spouse, intending to protect them. But when those facts are ultimately revealed or discovered, the deception can shake the marriage to the core. Harboring secrets can explode a marriage when the secrets are discovered, but it can also doom a marriage from the start. A long-held secret has a subversive, corrosive effect on trust and intimacy. The dance of intimacy depends on honesty; at the core of infidelity is a deceit that undermines faith in the marriage. We have to risk being honest with ourselves and with our partner. Otherwise, we will never get below the surface.

Intimacy means being willing to expose our truest self to another person and to receive their truest self in return. It requires risking vulnerability by letting the other person see us in all our imperfections. It allows the potential for deep acceptance in loving and being loved not only in spite of our flaws but, perhaps, because of them. This kind of intimacy is a brave risk. It's scary to trust another to receive us and be true. Intimacy is a self-reinforcing loop. The more you see me and accept me, the more I feel connected to you, see you, and accept you. It is often in our brokenness that we forge the deepest bonds.

When we returned from our jog and our conversation about deceit, I showered and got ready to pick up Timmy for his soccer game. Matt came upstairs, looking a bit sheepish as he handed me a page with an email printed on it. He told me he had received it the day before and shrugged his apology for not sharing it with me. I took the page from him and read the email from "Sameri."

> Hello, Doctor.
>
> Did you get my note? I found your email anyway. I knew you when we were at Stanford. I've been living back East since then. Now that I'm back in the area, I'd love to find out if you are the same great guy I remember.
>
> How about we get together for piña coladas? Meet me at Perry's in Palo Alto on Sunday, say 4:00. I'll be the one with two piña coladas.
>
> Your Secret Admirer

I handed the page back to him, setting my face with a question mark of raised eyebrows and pursed lips. Of course, he had heard from her again. I appreciated him sharing the email and all of the earlier messages with me. My husband is a veiled person, introverted and quiet. He listens intensely and may not share his thoughts. When he does speak, people are often surprised by the depth of his attention and understanding. Over time, he had revealed more and more of himself to me. I knew a part of him would have liked to accept the invitation and indulge the secret.

He pondered the email in his hand. He was still worried that it was a setup, which, of course, it was. But I could tell he was hopeful that it wasn't.

"I don't know what to do."

"Well," I said, matter-of-factly, "I think you need to meet her and put an end to this whole thing."

My response surprised him. He quietly considered, and I could see he was torn.

"If you want, I will go with you," I offered.

"No!" he answered a little too quickly. "She'll probably leave if she sees you there."

"Well, she seems to have a lot of information about you, including tracking down your email. She must know that you're married. And if she's from Stanford, she probably knows you're married to me. I wonder if I know her."

We brainstormed a little more together and agreed that he would go to meet her while I waited for him at my office nearby. He replied to her email and confirmed the meeting: Sunday at 4:00 at Perry's. I was relieved to bring the deception to an end and hopeful Matt would be pleasantly surprised, although now I could see the risk.

> ***The dance of intimacy depends on honesty; at the core of infidelity is a deceit that undermines faith in the marriage.***

Reflection

- How much truth is necessary to a good marriage, to our good marriage?
- What types of untruths are permissible for us?

- What are the secrets I keep from my partner? Would these same secrets be okay for my partner to keep from me?
- Do I feel differently about emotional infidelity and sexual infidelity?
- What would I do if I discovered my partner had had an affair? Do I believe our marriage could recover? Why or why not?

9

REVELATION

Sunday afternoon

Finally, the time had arrived. Will he, or won't he? I was sitting at a small table in the back of Perry's in downtown Palo Alto, waiting to see. The bar was dimly lit and nearly empty on a Sunday afternoon. It was an upscale hive of activity most nights, but it seemed a bit tawdry with the sun shining bright outside, the glaring light of day on what should be done only in shadow.

Once Matt had agreed to meet his secret admirer, my shadow came out to play, the side of myself that I didn't allow into the light. She was a secretly wanton woman, craving excitement and risk. We had great fun shopping that afternoon, my shadow and I. We looked through the sale racks, thinking, *What would I never wear?* and selecting lingerie, leopard prints, big hoop earrings, and frivolous, frolicking, almost costume clothing at bargain prices. The final stroke of brilliance was stopping at the beauty salon to have my hair styled, feathered around my face in a style I had only tried once before in high school.

My office was empty on a Sunday afternoon, so it became my dress-up room. I tried to shed my internalized inhibitions and cultural constraints as I changed into my costume: my very first push-up bra, silky unders, the sheer leopard print dress with a few top and bottom buttons left undone, strappy shoes, and a little too much makeup. I had created a living version of my alter ego to invite Matt's seduction—and my own. The wardrobe change helped shift my inner awareness as well. Self-consciously stepping out onto the street, I looked around, sure I would be arrested. But then I realized lots of women dress like this every day, just not me. I walked the couple blocks downtown to our rendezvous.

Arriving early, I tried to get comfortable at the bar, but there was something inherently uncomfortable about the place and the whole illicit scene. I had never done anything like this before. Although I had donned leopard spots on a new sheer cotton dress, I was not sure I could actually grow into them. The new underwire bra dug into my ribs, and the silk panties felt cool under my seat. How do you entice a man into an affair? I've seen it done in the movies, and even then, it seems so cheap. Show a little leg, flutter the lashes, run a finger across his arm, linger over the glass, smile, pout, but don't use too many words. Vapid, vacuous, vacant, vampy. Even as an act, it doesn't sound very interesting. But apparently, it is what men want at some level—an accepting, admiring, attractive angel, totally adoring and therefore totally adorable.

This was not my style. In high school, I actually had a small part as a call girl in the school play. How I got cast for that part is beyond me. I only had a few lines, but they caught in my throat as I tried to get them out in the high-pitched ditzy voice our drama teacher expected. That was the closest I had ever come to playing the adoring, alluring femme fatale.

When the waitress approached, unaware of the drama unfolding, I ordered two piña coladas.

"Sorry, we don't make 'em," she said and waited for a second choice.

For her, this was simply business as usual. For me, an essential element of the charade was lost.

"Two margaritas will do, thank you." I smiled thinly, wondering, *What—too cliché? Is it too much trouble to stock a little coconut syrup and pineapple juice? Is the combination too likely to attract the wrong element, the vapid and vampy?*

Okay, breathe, I coaxed myself. *You have set this up, and now it is time to relax and enjoy it.* Soon, it would be out of my hands and up to him to engage, to take the reins. I would be on the receiving end, where I have often been before, in the more passive role, waiting and responding. The last few days had been a lovely departure, to be the one initiating, inviting, enticing, entrapping. It was much easier anonymously, but now we would meet face to face. At four o'clock, I took one last deep breath.

Matt came around the corner of the bar, the tell-tale spring in his step. He was tall and casual but alert, feigning nonchalance but clearly on edge. Mine was the only occupied table, with the two frothy drinks in plain view. He approached, still trying and failing to maintain some appearance of diffidence as he walked toward destiny. I kept my eyes totally focused on his, inviting him closer, closer, closer. He smiled vaguely. Then a shadow crossed his face, a question and then a shock. All semblance of poise vanished. He stared, stunned, then dropped into the seat opposite me with a thud. He sat very still, his mind in overdrive, and I could see him replaying the events of the past week in rapid sequence, trying to reorganize his thinking, grasping for some missed clue.

"Is this a test? What if I hadn't told you?" His voice was rising. Fear and guilt began to merge into anger.

"It would still be me sitting here." I gave him time to adjust. He needed it. His head was almost spinning on its axis. I held his gaze and raised my glass—a toast to open the affair. He was clearly ready for a drink but unsure what would follow, and that of course, was up to him.

We shared a moment's reprieve in the cool tartness of the tequila and lime. The weight of his fear, guilt, and anger lifted and evaporated into the dim light. The sense of relief was perhaps accompanied by disappointment. There was a time when this reality—me sitting here inviting him to share a drink and what may follow—would well have met his expectations. But now? He was confused. A puzzle was emerging, a game. Would he be willing to play even if it was not a dangerous game? Even if it was to have an affair with his very own wife?

I set my glass down and took his hand.

"So, what did you tell your wife? Does she know you are here?" My crossed leg swung casually as I sat back and looked into his deep blue eyes, silently inviting, *I am here. Let's play.*

He stammered, still recovering from the shock. Tears pooled in the well of his eyelids and then spilled, a single stream over the familiar contour of his cheek. I squeezed his hand in mine. He had been struggling with such extreme emotions. He had been grappling with his understanding of himself as a husband, a lover, a man. And, now, in a moment, all of them had merged into one very simple prospect: an affair with his wife, long-time lover, and the woman he loves. Could it really be that simple? He took another sip, visibly relaxed, exhaled for the first time, and pondered the possibilities.

"Yes, she knows. She is waiting for me." Good, he was catching on and willing to play. His wife was out there, deceived. The woman before him was not his wife but wanted to be his mistress. I released his hand and ran my fingers along his arm.

"Well," I smiled and raised a curious brow, "what will you tell her?"

He was warming up by the minute.

"I will think of something."

He leaned forward and kissed me lightly on the lips, the salt and lime lovely.

"Do you remember the piña colada song?" I asked.

"Yeah, I've been humming it all day."

"And do you remember how it ends?" I teased.

"No, I never got that far."

We shared a laugh as I reminded him of the lyrics. The vapid conversation seemed somehow poignant, loaded with multiple meanings and no meaning at all, just an encounter of two people excited to see each other, as if for the first time in a long time, and to linger in each other's real presence.

The glasses were emptied, the calamari consumed. Where do we go from here? I invited him to spend the evening together knowing he couldn't. His wife was expecting him to call and then meet her to share his encounter with the secret admirer. But maybe one night this week, he could get away after dinner. He agreed to let me know by email. He stood to leave, and I stood to meet him in a full-body embrace. I kissed him, both of us full of longing and anticipation—a promise, a taste.

As he turned and walked more lightly into the early evening, I gathered myself in the shadows to venture back into reality, the various roles of wife, mother, lawyer, and others, but with a new one to be cultivated: paramour, "for love's sake."

> ***An encounter of two people excited to see each other, as if for the first time in a long time, and to linger in each other's real presence.***

Reflection

- What roles are we playing in our marriage?
- Are there roles or patterns I might be ready to let go?
- What would it risk for me to do so? Growth requires a temporary suspension of security.
- Are we both equally open to change in our relationship? Is that important to me? To us?

10

SHADOW DANCE

Sunday evening

I left the bar feeling giddy with relief and excitement. Despite Matt's trepidation during the lead up to our meeting, he had not reacted at the moment of revelation with anger or suspicion that I might have been trying to trap him. I hadn't even considered that idea until my friend's reaction over coffee, but then I could see it was a real possibility. The truth was I knew my husband, trusted that he would actually love to play, and felt confident that he also needed this release. Matt had grown into our relationship and his female-dominant psychology profession by leaning into his feminine side. He had perhaps suppressed his own masculine power and sexuality, which, for him, was also tied up with shame and guilt from his Catholic upbringing.

When faced with the seduction, he reacted with anxiety and paranoia that he was being set up for a shameful exposure.

I never thought it would go this far before he caught on. This was the fantasy or play he had invited just the week before. I was simply making things up as I went along, building toward this face-to-face meeting. The ruse was not risk free, and I would not recommend trying this at home. Although I felt like I was in control, Matt could have responded in any number of ways I hadn't even imagined. I had considered that he might not share the messages with me, but, honestly, I figured that, if he didn't, it would just show that he needed it more than I thought he did. At the end of the day, it would be me sitting there inviting him to play. Fortunately, he chose to engage and we were now coconspirators in the game.

I wondered whether there was a risk of inviting a real affair. I decided that was always a risk, but not opening ourselves to one another would be much more dangerous. Over time, I had unconsciously constructed an outward sexual persona tangled up in external judgments about myself as a woman, a wife, and a lawyer that left my inner self neglected and silenced. These are just the kind of unconscious pulls that can erupt into an affair. When my repressed feminine shadow broke through, my impulse was toward Matt, toward our marriage, rather than toward an outside romantic experience. When Matt was feeling confused and vulnerable to the threatened seduction, he turned to me, to our marriage, for advice and support. Even as we were the intimate partners binding and frustrating each other, we were also the most trusted and wise confidants to one another. That was a critical turn toward the marriage as our midlife walls were closing in.

We were entering into a new experience, rejuvenating and healing at the same time. What had begun as a whim had become an essential exploration and a great release for me to awaken my shadow, which I had long resisted, afraid she would undermine my professional credibility and personal authority. Matt's paranoid reaction spoke to his desire for affirmation through sexuality and his less conscious sense of shame. I was hoping to bring out the wolf in Matt, to give it permission to emerge. I was surprised to find the she-wolf in myself, longing for her own expression.

In my musing, I recalled a story from *Soul Mates* by Thomas Moore. It was a Native American story about a young Cochiti girl living in the village who was much sought after for her beauty, as well as her artistic skills. She had her pick of the men of the village to be her husband, but she was not interested in any of them. She rebuffed their advances and kept her attention on her weaving. Then Coyote came to court her, donning a human costume of beautiful finery. He charmed her with his dance and offered her five currants in his palm. She gave herself to him, and they were soon married and bore small coyote children.

I loved the image of inviting the wolf, of going beyond the logistics of a marriage to find the magic. I wanted to evoke the myth lying deep in the lover's heart. I had donned my costume and charmed Matt with my dance. I had offered my sensual self in a completely new way. As much as we appreciate the productive, predictable partner in life, can we still see the wild, primitive, even magical energy underneath the sheep's clothing? Can we allow our lover to run a little wild in the safety of our embrace? Can we surrender to the force of their magic? Can we hold the currants in one hand to charm them as we use the other hand for the mundane business of making a living and building a home?

A few days after our clandestine meeting, I was getting ready to head out the door to drop Timmy at school. As I finished preparing breakfast and lunch, I mused about setting up another rendezvous.

"Matt?" I called across the house. "I've got a meeting this evening, after dinner at 7:30."

He was also rushing around to get out the door.

"Okay," he paused, catching on. "I'm supposed to meet Dave tonight. I guess Cass can keep an eye on Timmy for a couple hours."

I smiled, looking forward to a little dalliance after dinner.

That evening, Timmy cleared the table—under protest, of course—and we enlisted Cassedy to be in charge for the evening. I spent a little extra time getting ready for my meeting, spritzing seldom-used perfume and donning a new blouse with a plunging neckline. A gentle excitement fluttered below my heart. Matt had already left to meet his buddy.

Arriving at a hip downtown restaurant as younger couples began their evenings, I smoothed the new blouse over my hips and wriggled a little to release the nerves of this still unfamiliar embodiment of feminine allure. I spotted him, sitting alone, eyes on me and waiting. I smiled genuinely. He stood to greet me with a kiss and strong embrace and gallantly pulled out the chair for me. We both breathed a release of the familiar and inhaled the fragrance of the new. We sat together, gently toying with each other's hands—renewed tenderness. We ordered cognac and a chocolate mousse with raspberries—extravagance to share. Our conversation was light. Our silences were pleasant. Our touches were delicious. When it was time to go, we promised to get together for a longer time, perhaps a weekend getaway very soon. Then we kissed goodbye because we each had to get back to our home and family.

I had often wondered how people found time for an affair. With a career, three children at varying stages of narcissistic demands, involvement in community and professional organizations, extended family commitments, among any number of distractions—really, where did people find the time for extramarital activities? But now I got it. This affair was an energy boost, not a drain. The excitement and pure adventure of it added anticipation to every moment of the day. Thankfully, ours did not have the distress of betrayal, which would have been very difficult for me to bear. In our private affair, I could engage freely, without threatening the marriage and actually acting in service of our intimacy. As our affair continued, I often found myself daydreaming about the last liaison or stopping to pick up a little something special for the next one. There was a new spice in my life, and it flavored all of my experience. The added logistics were well worth it.

Our domestic life ground along as usual. The ritual family dinner—Matt did the cooking of course—proceeded on schedule. Everyone was at the table at 6:00 sharp. The conversation around the meal was taken up with sharing our days and the children's activities, as well as planning for upcoming events. But, even in the old routine, there was a new sparkle of appreciation and anticipation.

"I am going to the family law conference next weekend in Monterey," I told Matt matter-of-factly. "I'll be gone from Saturday morning to Sunday about 3. What's your schedule?"

He paused, looking for clues, and then answered, "I've got the boys' weekend up north. I was planning to leave early Saturday for the weekend."

Normally, I would have been frustrated with the lack of planning and the burden of making arrangements for the kids. Instead, I replied almost cheerfully.

"Well, I will see if my mom can come for the weekend. When will you be back?"

"Sunday evening."

The following Saturday morning, I packed up my suitcase, met my mother at the door with a list of instructions, and then took off for my conference. Matt had already left for his boys' getaway. I felt tickled as I drove away from the house.

I noticed his car waiting when I parked on the street just around the corner from our house. Matt came over and greeted me with a hug and a kiss and helped me with my overnight bag. I had booked a room at a romantic little B&B on the coast. We would have two luxurious days together, the first since our meeting at Perry's a few months before. I rolled down the window and let the breeze blow through my hair as Matt played classic rock on the car stereo. We held hands across the console but didn't share many words, each enjoying our own reverie.

Checking in at the B&B, I felt a little guilty and then silly. The room was lovely, with a big four-poster bed, antique furnishings, and a large stone fireplace. Once the door was closed behind us, we fell into a desperate embrace and let the excitement release into a passionate encounter, leaving us both smiling and spent. It was only 4:00. What would we do for the rest of the night?

We managed to while the time away over a complimentary bottle of wine and trivial conversation before heading to the oceanfront restaurant for dinner. I felt some tension as we searched for topics of conversation—not kids, not work, certainly not marriage. Those were not topics for an affair. Affairs require a level of intrigue, not the mundane. After all, the whole point is to get out of the routine, to allow the shadows to come out to play.

I sat looking out over the ocean, with the sun starting its descent toward the water, holding hands with my lover across the table.

"Of all the beaches you have been to, what is your favorite?" I asked.

He raised his eyebrows with interest.

"Hmm. I have spent a lot of time in Kauai. I love the sunsets from Ke'e Beach at the end of the road. They are magnificent, with a view of the NaPali coast. What about you?" he asked.

"I've spent time in Hawaii too," I mused. "I always love watching the sunset from Maui, dropping into the ocean between Lanai and Molokai. I also love the sunsets here along the California coast."

The conversation continued with beaches and sunset images drawn from around the country. Of course, we had been to many of the same places, but it was fun to share our recollections of favorite moments. That was a conversation that wouldn't normally have happened in a marriage. Still, I began to wonder whether the construct of the affair was sustainable or whether, at some point, it would even be interesting any longer. It seemed that the affair had opened us up to each other in certain neglected ways, but, at the same time, it did not allow us to bring all of our real selves to the conversation.

The next morning, we woke slowly, reorienting to the fantasy.

Taking up our roles, we played affair, like I used to play house as a kid. We languished over the bountiful breakfast delivered to our room, playing, teasing, and relaxing together but staying in character as clandestine lovers. After checking out, we strolled through the town's main street, picking up little gifts for each of our alter egos, clothing purchases slightly outside of our usual styles, a little closer cut or more brightly colored. The drive back over the mountain was quiet; it seemed the energy of the affair was winding down, folding back into the comfort and routine of our real but renewed marriage. We returned to my car and then to our shared home and put away the affair, to perhaps one day take out and play again.

My experience resonates with the writings of Esther Perel on infidelity: "Sometimes when we seek the gaze of another, it's not our partner we are turning away from, but the person we have become. We are not looking for another lover so much as another version of ourselves . . . So often, the most intoxicating 'other' that people discover in an affair is not a new partner; it's a new self."

Recognizing and then embodying my alter ego—my suppressed feminine sexuality—was an initial release with an exhilarating sense of freedom from old roles and stories. I was learning to integrate this aspect of myself into my marriage and my life. Initially playing a role in a costume, it was slowly becoming an authentic expression for me. Matt was doing the same with his masculinity. The marriage opened and softened to welcome these shadow parts of each of us, to expand beyond the bounds we had imposed for ourselves. The shadows had danced their day in the sun and were now allowed out of the closet. We fell back into the rhythm of our marriage, acknowledging the shadows as welcome parts of who we are and who we love. As we did, the facade of the affair became a little tiresome. It was cumbersome to keep up the artificial separation from our real marriage.

Through the affair, we were not only released from the roles of our marriage but also realized those constraints were of our own making. Elements of the affair leaked into the marriage. The clothes I had selected for their total incongruity with my persona within the marriage became part of the fabric of my authentic self. The new look triggered a memory of a thrill ride, an X-rated family vacation. Those parts of ourselves that we had hidden away and decided were not allowed had now found expression, and we were both better for it. It was a departure from the constraints of the marriage but, ultimately, with a safety net. It was the perfect affair.

> ***The marriage opened and softened to welcome these shadow parts of each of us, to expand beyond the bounds we had imposed for ourselves.***

Reflection

- How do I feel about the passion in our marriage?
- Do I feel a tension between stability or predictability and passion or spontaneity? How do we manage that tension in our relationship?

Practice

TOP TEN WAYS TO KEEP PASSION ALIVE

10. Attend to your personal mental and physical health to keep your energy and fitness up.
9. Take time for your personal grooming and wardrobe to continue to highlight your natural beauty and grace.
8. Set aside time for each other. In a busy schedule, schedule in time for priorities, including conversation and intimacy.
7. Create a welcoming and private space for your marriage, and create boundaries for children and others to protect your privacy.
6. Sparks are great, but to keep the fire burning, be consistent. It is much easier to rekindle than to start from cold coals.
5. Embrace spontaneity: Break the rules, add an element of surprise.
4. Kindle good old romance with flowers, unexpected gifts, notes, hugs, thoughtful support, and even cooking.
3. I'll say it again: Kiss early and often. Adopt kissing as a practice, a habit—hello, goodbye, goodnight. Practice makes perfect, maintains the connection, and can spark another fire.
2. Intimacy is crucial. Be attentive and connected. Silence your distractions and enjoy each other.
1. If all else fails, have an "affair"!

Resources:

Perel, Esther, *Mating in Captivity, Unlocking Erotic Intelligence*, Harper Collins (2006).

11

NEW GROWTH

Our marriage had become too small; the affair allowed us a release valve. The unexpressed parts of each of us had butted up against the walls of our container. Even as we each tried to hold the structure together, we chafed at the old rules and expectations. But we were able to step out of our marriage, out of the bounds we had created, to play with the affair. The brilliance was that it was still the two of us but freed from all the old stuff. We were able to experience each other and ourselves with new eyes. I wondered, at times, how Matt failed to recognize me in his secret admirer. It was almost as though his vision was veiled, as though he really did not want to see. When the scales fell from his eyes and the prospect of the affair was revealed, it was a jolt. He never saw it coming.

Funny thing: Those old efforts at conversation about restlessness, future plans, and new explorations that had been so difficult the years before began to unfold more easily. We had created more breathing space within our marriage. We were able to see each other differently, outside of the limited selves we had subscribed to. We didn't need to leave the marriage to explore another side of ourselves—but in a way, we had. The kind of frivolous flirtations, whimsical conversations, or even wanton sexual encounters that we had ruled out of the marriage found expression in the affair. The aspects of ourselves that we had each over time relegated to shadow were released in the freedom of play.

One of the powerful pulls of infidelity is the opportunity for these suppressed aspects of ourselves to come forward. Usually, that involves a third party, deception, broken promises, guilt, and tremendous heartbreak, which can damage the marriage beyond recovery. Our affair allowed us freedom, the realization of what we had repressed, and, rather than breaking our promises, we found a new and exciting connection back to one another.

We began to dream together again about what future years might bring. Tyler had two more years of college. He was thriving, playing baseball, and becoming engaged in his studies as he decided how he might move into the world. Cassedy would be off to college in two years, although she had not yet formulated plans for her studies beyond finishing high school. Timmy would start high school a year after his sister left home.

It suddenly dawned on me that we had a year between Cassedy graduating high school and Timmy starting. This realization created an opening for a new adventure. We felt high school was critical, but eighth grade seemed much more flexible. We could manage Timmy's education elsewhere, even home school him if necessary, and we could take a year away.

The idea of a sabbatical year began to grow. I could explore other work, teaching and writing, travel and home schooling. So many possibilities flooded in, so many opportunities for renewal. Matt also became excited about it, trusting that his work would be waiting for him when he returned. My situation was more complicated as a partner in a small law firm, but having tasted the potential, there was no turning back. Once the door of this sabbatical year opened as a real possibility, there was simply no closing it. To not take the year away would be a failure of imagination, of courage—a denial of a most inviting opportunity.

We explored and dreamed together now. My personal angst about wanting change was finding resolution, and Matt was totally engaged in the process. We considered numerous possibilities, including returning to Washington, DC, to work and study, or traveling the world while home schooling Timmy. Ultimately, these very ambitious plans faded from their own weight and the sense of exhaustion they brought forth. That spring, we took our usual week away to the island of Kauai. As we relaxed, immersed in nature and far from the madding crowd, we settled on a plan to spend the year on Kauai, doing nothing. I felt a sense of relief in a year open to rest and rejuvenation—a true sabbath. We checked out schools for Timmy and found a small private school on Kauai's North Shore, grades 7 to 12. We planned to rent our Palo Alto home and find a place to live on Kauai. We would both take the year off from our professional work to rest, reflect, and renew. We had two years to plan, budget, save, and negotiate our professional departures for our year away.

Those two years flew by. We celebrated Tyler's graduation from college and Cassedy's from high school. At the end of that summer, as Cassedy headed off to Oregon to start college, we took Timmy and left for Kauai. We literally departed from all the conventional wisdom about building security and left our various containers behind—home, careers, family, and professional identities. We created a real-life adventure that was like an oasis in the desert at that time of our lives. We made room for something completely new and surprising.

Timmy, a reluctant participant at first, ended up having an amazing coming of age year. On our flight to the island, I asked him how he was feeling about leaving. He schooled me, as only a 13-year-old can: "Uh, let's see, Mom. I spend a year living on Kauai and then I come back and am the coolest kid in high school. Yeah, I think I'm good."

He was welcomed by his eighth-grade Kauai classmates, where he found himself ahead in most of the academic subjects and also learned to shape a surfboard, work at a goat farm, and make fused glass. He joined the North Shore championship soccer team, learned to surf, and had the island as his playground. As a third child of working parents who was now an only child of nonworking parents, he got way more of our attention than he wanted. When we prodded him to do his homework or other tasks, he would complain that he was the only one that worked anymore.

Matt and I both nurtured neglected aspects of ourselves, which rejuvenated our zest for life and for each other. We dove into an intense yoga practice together. He also took up surfing and played golf almost daily. With the expanse of an entire year ahead, I had shipped several boxes of books to the island, as well as my sewing machine, which kept me happily occupied in these long-neglected pursuits. We watched the sunset each evening and felt the cycle of the year turn as the whales arrived in the winter and the albatross nested and then hatched their giant chicks to fledge by early summer. We hiked the NaPali Coast and kayaked its shore. Our condo was perched on the bluff, and we swam with sea turtles at the secluded beach below. We made many new friends in the local community among the parents of Timmy's classmates, our yoga community, and Matt's surf and golf buddies. We all thrived.

For me, this was my opportunity to pause, to get off the treadmill of constant motion our Palo Alto life had become—a time to explore new understandings of myself and my reason for being, which had been bubbling up for years. It was time to find my authentic internal compass, rather than conforming to patriarchal, religious, professional, or other cultural paradigms and their expectations of me.

Perhaps the seed of our sabbatical arose from the creative impulse of the affair. Perhaps the same transformative imperative was at the heart of both departures from convention. Either way, the conversation about how we could approach our future, individually and together, shifted and opened to new possibilities.

When we returned from our year away, we integrated aspects of our sabbatical into a new routine, as we had done with our "affair," including a daily yoga practice and regular surf sessions for Matt. I resigned from my law firm, started a new practice in dispute resolution, and began a master's program in transpersonal psychology. Matt restructured his practice to focus more on collaborative and conflict management roles. Our marriage was now large enough to hold both of our dreams and endless possibilities.

Marriage serves as a container for the dynamics of both people and the relationship itself. This container may be, at times, a place of safety and security, the comfort of home and hearth, a comfortable and well-worn shoe. The container may also be a fishbowl, exposing each partner's shadow and light, a place to reveal or heal ourselves—with no place to hide. At other times, it is a pressure cooker, forcing each person's psychological patterns and reactions to the surface.

The marriage percolates our emotional and psychological growth as we become each other's intimate partner, closest confidant, knowing the secrets and faults that we try to hide from others. When our insecurities and other emotional wounds bubble up, there is only one other person to project them onto, to rail against, to blame. And, of course, their stuff is bubbling up too. We are the foils for each other's foibles. We wouldn't have to confront certain truths about ourselves if it weren't for the forced intimacy of this pressure cooker. The container of our marriage had been holding all of that tension as we each dealt with our midlife growing pains. Yoga master teacher B. K. S. Iyengar taught that "when you want to get out of the pose is when the pose begins." In much the same way, when you want to get out of the marriage is when the marriage truly begins. We could both relate to this teaching, attempting to hold yoga poses for one more breath at a time, well beyond our self-imposed limitations. The commitment of the marriage allowed us to do this deep personal work within the safety of our trusted relationship.

Engaged and newlywed couples are often told that marriage takes work, but they have no idea what "work" really means. There will be times when marriage is hard, when you don't feel like being in the marriage anymore. This is likely when your chosen partner rubs you the wrong way, challenges you, and irritates you. This is the growth edge of the marriage, where the couple is forced to confront old patterns or beliefs. We are pushed beyond our comfort zone, and we don't like it. If we choose to shut down, we deny ourselves that opportunity to reexamine ourselves, to potentially come to a new understanding either affirming or modifying our views. If we leave the marriage at this point, we are likely to recreate the dynamic in a new relationship that will eventually arrive at this same point of tension, confronting us with the same issue in ourselves. As the adage says, *Wherever I go, there I am.* The work and potential of marriage confronts us with ourselves through the lens of our beloved's eyes—hopefully, a loving and accepting gaze, but still challenging.

Matt and I received a special wedding gift: a framed hand-embroidery that read, "Choose thy love; love thy choice." We took this wisdom to heart. We had made our choice and committed to love one another. There was nothing casual about this choice; we knew we would soon bring a child into the marriage. Matt quotes this gifted wisdom often when he speaks about our marriage as the best decision he ever made. To love our choice means that we choose each day to be in the marriage, whether we feel like it or not. We might think of love as an emotion, a feeling that comes and might go. In fact, love is a decision. There will be times when we don't feel love, when we don't even like our spouse. In those moments, we make a decision to love. It is a practice, a commitment to being true, to being loving, even in moments when it is hard. Marriage is not self-indulgent. Love takes us beyond our petty personal grievances or moods. Love expands our hearts to be able to respond in the moment to the other. This is the process of marriage as we work together and as the marriage works on us and for us.

> "What marriage offers—and what fidelity is meant to protect—is the possibility of moments when what we have chosen and what we desire are the same."
>
> —Wendell Berry, *The Body and the Earth (1976).*

Working with my divorcing clients, I have come to understand the many frustrations, life challenges, and changes that have brought the couples to a decision to separate. There is no single reason that people divorce; it is complicated. But, for me, the container metaphor holds true in many circumstances. The framework of the marriage that is constructed early on is, eventually and necessarily, outgrown. This outgrowth is a critical stage, challenging how the marriage will respond to either person's need to grow or shift or change. The marriage might be able to expand, to accommodate the necessary growth, or it may crack at the pressure and eventually break apart. Of course, partners don't usually grow at the same rate or in the same direction, which makes these shifts even more challenging.

Marriage can create an actual physical container in the form of a home. Whether a small apartment or a spacious single-family dwelling, our values and family culture are reflected in the way we inhabit our homes. One of the classic tensions in a marriage is the building of a new home, especially a dream home. I saw many couples seeking divorce on the heels of completing construction. At first, I thought the conflicts were based on preexisting issues that the couple simply sought to avoid by taking on the construction project. When we did our own remodel and eventually built our dream home, I realized a great deal of truth is revealed in literally constructing that container for the marriage and family.

When we bought our first home, it was the cheapest house on the market in Palo Alto, a tired 1,000 square feet with three small bedrooms and a single tiny bathroom. We dreamed of remodeling and adding space—creating a dining room, adding a master bedroom and bath, and extending a small room off the kitchen. For me, that room was a sunny breakfast nook or a den, but Matt claimed it as his office. For months, even into the eventual construction, I would mention the breakfast room, and he would counter with "my office." I'm not even sure what I had meant by "breakfast room"—a parlor or a sunny spot for a coffee? Matt's concept of an office was much more specific and functional, and he prevailed. It wasn't a big conflict, but it was enough for us to see that, to plan and build a home—or even to purchase and decorate one—the couple has to confront how and where they spend their time and how they each envision their life together. Facing those questions may bring conflicts to the surface. Of course, building a home can be highly stressful in itself, but I tend to think that marriages that don't survive the process are struggling with more foundational issues.

My parents' home became a metaphor for their marriage. They began their marriage overseas, with my father's active duty in the US Air Force. When they returned to California in the mid-1950s with three daughters under the age of three, they purchased a modest tract home on the outskirts of San Jose. My father was hired as a commercial airline pilot, and his schedule was unpredictable. He would be gone for a few days, then back home for a day or two, and then gone again, with no correlation to weekends or even holidays. The schedule changed each month and was peppered with his Air Force Reserve commitments. Our family home became a place of feminine chaos and creativity when my father was away. We four girls scattered projects everywhere and made easy meals of hot dogs or breakfast for dinner. My mother didn't like to cook any more than I did, but she didn't have a choice. As soon as we got the call that my father was on his way home, we quickly straightened up, put the projects away, and fell into a more orderly structure. While my father was home, we kept our rooms tidy, and my mother served a multiple-course dinner at the dining room table. We ate quietly with our best table manners. Once my father left again, we fell back into our creative chaos.

My mother seemed to enjoy her freedom and ease when he was away. My father may have felt confined, returning to our small home from his big world. He seemed angry and became increasingly frustrated and intolerant of our messes. He craved order and bristled at the signs of underlying chaos that we were unable to hide away. Tensions ran high when he was at home. When the family would get out of the house together for vacation or an outing for the day, he seemed to relax and enjoy all of us and his own role in the family much more.

When I was a teenager, my father took up gardening and started jogging, spending as much time outside the physical house as possible. Then, due to his seniority with the airline, he had the opportunity to train in and fly a newer aircraft, which would require him to commute from our family home in San Jose, California, to Las Vegas, Nevada, as his primary base. He accepted and soon set up a separate apartment there. He still returned home for longer breaks, but he clearly enjoyed the orderliness and control of his separate space. I visited him there with my younger sisters. My mother never did. She curled up more into her own familiar home. My father needed to expand. He encouraged her to join him, but she wouldn't. She resisted his new activities. She liked her old container—and her old husband.

In his early 50s, as I graduated from college, my father decided to leave the marriage. They had been married for 25 years. In the divorce, my mother kept the house, and she secluded herself in it. She never allowed it to expand beyond her comfort level, and she became reclusive for several years. The house, like the marriage, had been both a security and a confinement for her. Slowly, it became old and worn, falling into disrepair. Twenty-five years after the divorce, she moved into a fresh space, where she became her own person and more at peace with herself.

I was fascinated by marriage, amazed that couples would promise their entire life to another human being, as though it were the most natural thing in the world. People who were deathly afraid of spiders or heights would readily pronounce "I do" to a daunting list of eternal vows. I was equally fascinated by divorce—how, in time, that same couple arrived at a point of mutual disillusionment or singular contempt, deciding to end the marriage. There were other reasons for my interest in family law, such as the relationship dynamics, the rise and fall of a marriage, the various business and financial interests, and how to deal with them under California's community property laws. I was intrigued by social change in family relationships, cohabitation, premarital agreements, same-sex partnerships and then marriages, parentage, and surrogacy. It was a constantly evolving social, emotional, and financial landscape.

As time went on, I came to realize that I also had a more personal motive in my work. I wanted to help couples through the gauntlet of divorce. But, at a deeper level, I sought to heal my own parents' divorce. I was 22 years old and had just graduated from college when my father decided to leave. Although I knew they had problems, I never thought my parents would separate. I represented both husbands and wives, who, at times, represented my parents to me. I saw my father in the midlife husband seeing his life passing him by and saw my mother in the long-suffering housewife watching her daughters embark on paths unavailable to her. Through working with these clients, I sought to understand and forgive my father for leaving and to support and empower my mother in creating an independent life.

The growth process and the challenge it presents to marriage never end. While divorce rates have historically declined as couples age, the divorce rate for couples over age 50 has doubled over the last 25 years. I have worked with couples married for 40 and even 50 years who chose to spend their golden years apart. I represented two women at about the same time, one a devout Catholic and one a devout Mormon. They were each leaving a 40-year marriage. Each woman had been unhappy for many years but felt that suffering in silence was what their faith and vows required of them. Late in life, both women received essential encouragement—one from her minister, the other from her adult children—to consider separation. The women found new peace and joy in a much simplified—but still deeply religious—single life.

In previous generations, older couples, even if they were not totally satisfied in the marriage, were not expecting to live much longer. They were more comfortable settling in for their final years together. As demographics and life expectancies have shifted, couples at age 60 have realized that they may have 20 to 30 more years to live. They more critically examine whether they want to spend those years in their marriage. In fact, some commentators attribute the higher modern divorce rate to our longer lifespan, arguing that marriages were never meant to last for 40-plus years.

Over time, one partner may come to a new essential understanding of himself or herself that rocks the marriage. A powerful example is sexual orientation. Early in my practice, I represented a woman who sought divorce from her husband of 20 years to pursue a relationship with her new female partner, who was also leaving a long-term marriage. My client's husband was hostile and difficult in the divorce, but I was surprised by my client's own intense anger. Although she was upset with her husband, I think she may have been more embittered by her circumstances and having denied her truth for so many years. More recently, I mediated the divorce of another couple where the husband came out as gay after 40 years of marriage. He loved his wife and hoped to maintain a friendship with her after the divorce, but it was too painful for her, and she wanted no further relationship. Even with good intentions, these dramatic shifts reverberate in the lives of both partners, and they can be difficult to integrate. Greater social awareness and gender fluidity may help navigate these changes. I know a young married couple where one of the partners is transitioning and they are staying together.

In retirement, like the recent COVID-19 confinement, the couple often finds themselves in closer quarters, sharing more time together now that one or both of them are no longer working outside the home. This disrupts their usual rhythm of time apart during the day. Tensions that have been brewing for years were tolerated because the couple didn't spend much of their day together. When the couple is contained in the home together for days on end, those tensions bubble over. Their former avoidance comes home to roost.

Faced with their own aging and mortality, many people find that their priorities change. I have represented more than one couple who, late in life, moved in opposite directions. The husband, in my cases, sought more adventure, physical exertion, and risk, while the wife sought more solitude and introspection. Although it is not easy, it is possible to restructure the marriage to allow and even support these divergent pursuits. This is especially true if the couple has developed skills for reflecting and reconciling their differences along the way. If they are going to stay together, as with earlier shifts in the marriage, the couple may need to recreate the marriage and adopt a different approach for this new chapter of life.

Marriage is a dynamic flow, navigating constant change. It is part of the ebb and flow of life, like waves on the shore. We can be confident that the tide will turn. The difficulty of today will become the wisdom of tomorrow. When all seems well and calm, enjoy it, because it is not likely to last.

Our midlife wave rode a rising tide of discontent and disconnection, of vulnerability and reconciliation. Our marriage of two good people, deeply caring for each other, struggled to surf this wave. We took a wild ride—creatively, skillfully, lovingly. But the ride ends; the wave crashes and recedes back into the ocean. We keep paddling back out, calmly scanning for the next wave. And it will come.

> ***When you want to get out of the marriage is when the marriage truly begins.***

Reflection

- Does our relationship support my individual growth? How so?
- Do I support my partner's growth? How so?
- What pressures have we faced from within our marriage?
- What challenges have we confronted from outside our marriage?
- What supports have we found in managing these challenges?

12

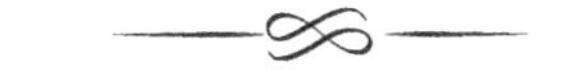

THE DEPTHS

As we have seen, there are pressures from within the marriage. The evolving values, desires, and priorities of the two partners can strain the marriage container. There are also massive pressures from outside the marriage that can shatter it altogether. Over the course of a lifetime together, all couples will face one or more devastating events—the loss of loved ones, serious illness or disability, economic disaster, and, increasingly, natural disaster. These are the times that truly test the mettle of a marriage. All of the resources of each partner and of the marriage itself will be necessary to survive these trials.

I represented a woman who, at age 50, suffered a massive stroke and was left severely disabled. At that same time, I represented a client whose partner, in her early 50s, was struck with a disabling spinal cord injury. Each of these 25-year marriages was jolted by the immediate demands and then long-term effects of one partner's sudden physical disability. Despite the best intentions of everyone involved, neither marriage could survive. Even when the blow comes from outside the marriage, couples turn toward each other, their closest confidant, whether in rage, blame, desperation, or grief. It is sometimes more than a marriage can endure.

30th year

It is the call in the middle of the night that every parent dreads. Like other parents, I had carried a constant prayer in my heart for 30 years to keep my children safe. At 3:15 a.m. one Sunday morning, the gentle harp tone of my cell phone startled me out of a deep sleep. I answered before I had fully awakened.

"Hello?"

"Sherry, hey. This is Brian. Uh, Timmy had an accident. It's pretty bad."

Blinking fog from my brain, I said, "What happened? Where are you?"

Seeing me bolt upright in the bed, Matt rose from the other side of the bed, already pulling on his clothes.

"We were coming back from the party. I was on my bike, and Timmy had his skateboard. I was ahead of him on this hill, and then his skateboard came flying by me. He was down. He hit his head, and it's pretty bad. The paramedics are here."

"How bad?" The fog was now clearing, and I was sorting for essential information.

"Well, he's unconscious, and he has blood coming out of his nose and ear. They're going to airlift him over the hill to Valley Medical."

"Honey, we need to go now," I called to Matt who I could hear in the kitchen packing things up. "Brian, where are you?"

"In Capitola. The paramedics are leaving soon. I gave them your cell."

"Okay, tell them we are leaving now and will meet them at the hospital."

"Okay." His voice indicated that he was clearly not okay.

I hung up and steeled myself against the wave of pure panic. *NO!* everything in me was screaming. But it is amazing what a locked jaw and singular focus can withstand—or, at least, forestall. I stuffed my books and laptop into my bag as I called to Matt, clear and calm, struggling for control of my voice.

"Timmy fell and hit his head—hard. He has blood coming from his nose and ear. They are taking him to Valley Med. We can meet him there."

The need for immediate action helped quell the rising panic. I struggled to put the pieces together as I threw on clothes and shoes. Matt and I were in Santa Cruz for the weekend. The evening before, we had stopped in at 20-year-old Timmy's small rented house. Timmy was a sophomore at UC Santa Cruz majoring in math and was working hard to become fluent in German so that he could attend Frei University in Berlin the next year. He had just been told he was admitted to the program, and we had wanted to congratulate him. The boys were going to a party that night, a few miles away, and we headed off to the movies, knowing we would have more time to talk with him in the morning. Timmy told us he was not that interested in the party but was going as Brian's wingman.

I grabbed my phone and hit redial.

"Hello."

"Brian, where are you? Do you want to come with us to the hospital?" I demanded in my take-action mode.

"Yeah. Uh, I'm walking on Portola with my bike."

"Okay." He was on our way, and we agreed to pick him up in a few minutes.

We found Brian easily. Matt packed his bike into the back of the car, and we headed over the hill. It was about a 40-minute drive over Highway 17, winding through the mountains from Santa Cruz to San Jose. Once we were in the car, the immediate action ceased, and the panic returned. I repeated Timmy's name in a mantra: "Timmy, Timmy, Timmy, Timmy." I was reminded of doing the same thing 20 years earlier. We had been following an ambulance carrying infant Timmy after he had a grand mal seizure, and I had chanted his name all the way to the hospital. It served to calm me, occupy my mind, and voice my urgent prayer, which had been answered those many years ago. Now, it had a similar effect, holding insanity at bay while I tried to believe there was some hope that Timmy could be alright.

Unable to convince myself, I turned to Matt and said matter-of-factly, "Our lives have just irrevocably changed." He silently acknowledged that truth with his eyes and looked back to the road, the intensity of the drive thankfully occupying his full attention.

Brian was sitting stunned in the backseat. The little redhead had been Timmy's best friend since kindergarten. Now, as college students, they shared the small house in Santa Cruz. I turned to face him.

"Brian, this is not your fault." Waiting for eye contact, I calmly continued. "Don't even go there. Timmy is a big boy. You are not responsible for this. Do you understand?"

His quiet acquiescence confirmed that he had, in fact, gone there and that he needed exactly this admonishment. He nodded to convince himself.

As we reached the summit, I allowed myself to think about the next few hours and who we should contact. Although it was necessary, spreading the news beyond this circle of three made it more devastatingly real. I reached for my phone and told Matt I would call Tyler, Timmy's big brother by almost 10 years, and Pam, Matt's sister and an ICU nurse. The calls were brief. There was not much information to share. But even being awakened at this hour of the night, they both understood the gravity and promised to meet us at the hospital.

We arrived at Valley Medical's Emergency entrance at 4:00 a.m. in the ragged daze of alarmed parents. The nurse told us that Timmy had also just arrived, which sounded somehow reassuringly normal. He would be seen by the trauma doctor, and she would let us know as soon as we could see him. More time to wait, to breathe, and to pray. Tyler arrived, and then Pam joined the vigil. We were sitting together in near silence when the trauma doctor came in.

After brief introductions, he gave us a grave look that you never want to see a doctor give.

"It is very serious. He may not make it."

As he explained the nature of the severe head trauma and brain stem injury, I listened intently, searching for hints of hope, but there were none.

"In the best case, if he survives, he will have very limited recovery."

And then I didn't know what to pray for. He told us they had given Timmy drugs to try to reduce the swelling of his brain and that, now, we needed to wait.

"Wait for what?" I asked.

"To see if the drugs are having any effect," the doctor responded, then added, "To see if he will declare himself."

I nodded numbly, not knowing what that meant but accepting that I would understand soon enough. We waited. It was almost 7:00 a.m. by the time the nurse said we could see Timmy. He had not responded to the drug. There was no change.

Matt and I spent the day hovering at Timmy's bedside, with our son connected to various machines helping to keep him alive. He appeared to be sleeping peacefully, but we had no idea what was happening inside his body or mind.

At 1:30 that afternoon, Timmy declared himself.

Matt was standing over one side of the bed as I perched on the other side, holding Timmy's hand and occasionally gently stroking the stubbly close-cut hair on his precious head. Otherwise motionless, Timmy's breath rose and fell rhythmically with the help of the ventilator.

Suddenly, the sound was broken by three short panting exhales and then silence. Matt and I exchanged looks of alarm and concern—parental looks. The monitor alarms began to beep and buzz, inciting a rush of nurses into a flurry of activity—pressing buttons and consulting machines. After almost an hour, his vitals were stabilized, and the life support equipment was restored to its rhythmic hum. But Timmy was gone.

The next morning, Matt and I sat together with the neurosurgeon in a small reception room off the hospital trauma unit as he explained brain stem death and Timmy's inability to recover. I was listening intently through a fog of disbelief. I needed to understand exactly what had happened to my son, grasping for any straw of hope. The doctor was taking great pains to answer all of our questions, wanting to provide some comfort. At some point, he stopped, nodded toward Matt, and quietly asked me, "Is he going to be okay?"

I looked over to see my husband slumped forward, head in hands, a pool of grief. *In what universe is he ever going to be okay?!* I thought. He has just been told his youngest child, his sweet boy, is gone. At the same time, I thought, *Of course, he is going to be okay; we are going to be okay because we have no choice and because we have each other.* What neither of us could possibly bear alone, we could bear together. Our marriage would hold us.

My ring of fire image, of moving through and surviving difficult and even threatening change, didn't hold up. Timmy's death completely shattered our lives, bringing down all the walls. Everything that we believed about life, about ourselves, and about the world was pulled out from under us. Each of our psyches had to be reconstructed from the ground up. *What is true? What is life? Where is my son now? Who am I now? What is the point? What meaning can I conjure from this?*

As we each grasped for threads, struggled for handholds, we also held the weight of the other's very individual and separate grief. We knew from prior experience that each partner may grieve quite differently. We had been together through the loss of two of our nephews and both of our fathers. We had sat with friends grieving the loss of their child. In those losses, we had been able to stay connected and support each other. But now we were both laid bare.

We leaned into every support we had, individually and as a couple. Although they were living independent adult lives, Tyler and Cassedy returned home to hold a form of family together. Our extended family of sisters, brothers, and God-family supported us. Our dear friends arrived with the best gift—their presence—as we began to plan rituals and services that no parent should ever have to plan. Timmy's friends inhabited our home, as they had in their teenage years, and conjured a sense of his presence in their grief and remembrance. Our yoga practice, our faith community, our family, and our marriage guided us through those early days, one uncertain step at a time, as we made a way forward into a complete unknown.

Matt and I were in a tender trance, together and most deeply alone. We gathered with family and reached out to our dearest friends, but we were isolated within the surreality that our youngest son was dying. We moved through the rituals of the next weeks in shock. Fortunately, we were both able to take time away from work to tend to our broken hearts. Our home was filled with family and friends, but the upper room was reserved as a sanctuary for our intimate grief. I spent the early days downstairs at our dining room table surrounded by friends and family, sharing stories and photos and planning for the rituals to come. This is where my extroverted soul found comfort. Matt spent most of his time upstairs, alone and in deep, solitary grief. I was very aware of him. I knew how shattered he was. I joined him upstairs at times, as did a few close friends who were willing to stand the heat of his despair. We didn't talk much. We slept well, a blessed escape.

Caring for my adult son and daughter and Timmy's dear shattered friends in their open grief and being present to Matt's all-consuming sadness required that I hold my own grief somewhat apart. In fact, my own grief was held in each of theirs; mothering them nurtured me as well. The bond of love overcame the depth of our individual griefs as we gathered to do the work of remembrance. It was a spiritual process and very human, guided and blessed by a larger compassion.

Three days after Timmy had left his body, Matt and I were again at his bedside, waiting to say goodbye to our son's body, to walk him to the operating room. It sounded so civilized, sterile, and healing. But no, this surgery would remove his vital organs, place them in containers to be preserved. They would then be transported to various other ORs, where doctors waited to transplant them into other patients' bodies.

We weren't thinking of that reality as we stood vigil at his bedside, watching him seemingly sleeping. We walked the gurney down the hall to the OR. As we went through the doors to the vestibule, I realized the truly terrible nature of this surgery, this deconstruction of my son's body. I wanted to stop it, to save him, to keep him. But I let him go, and the doors closed behind him.

We walked like zombies to the car. Matt put on a beautiful, haunting, repetitive chant: "Returning, returning, returning to the Mother of us all." We listened and cried as we drove the half hour home. We arrived at about 1:00 a.m. As we parked on the street, we were touched to see the entire house alight with candles. It was piercingly beautiful and sad. There were candles on the front fence, on the patio, at the front doorstep. As we entered through the living room and into the family room, candlelight was the only source of light. It was vigil, lovely and haunting. Tyler and Cassedy, our siblings, a few of our friends, and some of Timmy's friends greeted us as we gathered in the gentle light, in the middle of that dark night. Matt put on the chant, the simple repetition of "Returning, returning, returning to the Mother of us all." We sat together in the semi-dark, chanting, crying, praying, and holding silence while Timmy's body was in surgery.

In the morning, it was over. My body was weighed down with grief. I could barely lift my head, much less my body. I laid catatonic, sleeping on and off throughout the day. At times, I heard voices downstairs and thought that I should get up and join them—but the thought did not have the power to move me. I felt no obligation to do anything other than tend my own broken heart.

At about 4:00 in the afternoon, I sensed a glimmer of light—perhaps from the window, perhaps from somewhere beyond. I thought, *I could get up and shower and go downstairs.* I considered dismissing it and pulling the covers back over my head, as I had done many times already that day. But there was the invitation, the possibility of rising. In that moment, I realized I had a choice. I could shut out the glimmer. But some part of me recognized that the opening might not last and that I needed to move toward the light when it appeared, however faint. I opened the covers of my cocoon and slowly, gently moved my body forward, toward the light. That became a pivotal moment—choosing the light when it presented itself. It was a sacrifice of the sadness to the possibility of something else—hope.

At the end of the week, as we finalized plans for Timmy's celebration of life, Matt joined us at the dining table to say that he wanted to open Timmy's memorial with a chant: "Atha yoga anushasanam." Our teacher, Bhavani Maki, translates this yoga sutra as, "It has taken us our entire lives to arrive at this moment." Everything that has come before has prepared us for this moment. All of our prior struggles, experience, losses, and wisdom come to bear in this moment. A few days later, Matt and I led this opening chant together for the couple hundred people gathered in the high school outdoor amphitheater. This moment, right here, right now, is the invitation, and everything that has come before brings us to this moment. The marriage that Matt and I had created painstakingly over the years had become a strength, a third body, that could hold both of us when we had nothing left to give.

> "Grief never ends . . . But it changes. It's a passage, not a place to stay. Grief is not a sign of weakness, nor a lack of faith . . . It is the price of love."
>
> —*Unknown*

The death of a child is a devastating loss for anyone, and it is even more difficult for a marriage. For the marriage to survive, both partners need to work through their own grief while, at the same time, allowing space for the other to grieve. If the partners blame themselves or the other for the loss, grief becomes not only isolating but also conflicted. Other complications surrounding the death—an accident, illness, or suicide—can make it even more difficult for the couple to find compassion for one another. Some limited research and plenty of anecdotal evidence tells us that many couples—perhaps as many as 80 percent—separate after the death of a child. The pain of being together is too much to bear.

My grief was active. I threw myself into planning the ceremonies, establishing communication for his friends, and setting up a charitable fund. Slowly, I sorted through his room, finding treasures hidden there. I collected the records from his accident. Eventually I walked to the place of the accident and sat on my nearby mourning bench. Matt's grief was a solitary, silent, pervasive sadness. He didn't want to talk; he couldn't. The grief was overwhelming. When I stopped moving, I could find him there, and we could hold each other in the shared love and profound loss of our son. In that silent embrace, we were held within the strength of our marriage, in everything that had gone before, to be with the utterly unknown.

Over the next months, we continued to create rituals, gathering with friends and scattering Timmy's ashes in various places: Kauai at his six-month anniversary, the Oregon coast for his one-year anniversary, and the ginkgo tree planted for him at the Frei University in Berlin the following year. Each time, we tapped into new feelings of grief expressed through poems and songs that spoke to us in the moment. Tyler and Cassedy were intimate partners in our grief. They reflected aspects of each of us in their feelings and had their own grieving process as well.

Timmy's friends also continued to gather and included us in their own rituals and remembrances as they finished college, took jobs, and moved on with their lives. Tyler and Cassedy have both married, developed careers, and have children of their own. New life helps heal the loss. From spending time with Timmy in Santa Cruz, we eventually found a new home for ourselves not far from the little house where Timmy lived his last days. We walk often past the bluff where we had his paddle out and down the hill where he took his last fall. We embrace his memory, the joy and zest for life he exuded. I have a deep trust that Timmy continues in some way on his own unique journey. For Matt it is harder. As we walk together, we each continue our integration of Timmy's life and death in our own ways.

What neither of us could possibly bear alone,
we could bear together.
Our marriage would hold us.

Reflections

Often, in offering condolences, people would say, "I can't imagine." And of course, they can't and hopefully will never have to. But what do we know about our own emotional (sadness, anger, guilt) and psychological (gratitude, resentment, blame) reactions to loss and how they might play out in our relationship?

- What do I know about how I grieve? What do I need from my partner to allow myself to grieve?
- What do I know about how my partner grieves? What might my partner need from me in grief?
- How are our needs in deep loss different?
- What are my beliefs about death and after-life? How do my beliefs impact my grief process?

THE THIRD BODY

Robert Bly

A man and a woman sit near each other,
And they do not long
At the moment to be older, or younger,
Nor born in any other nation, time, or place.
They are content to be where they are,
Talking or not talking.
Their breaths together feed someone whom
We do not know.
They obey a third body that they share in common.
They have made a promise to love that body.
Age may come, parting may come,
Death will come.
A man and a woman sit near each other;
As they breathe, they feel someone we do not know,
Someone we know of, whom we have never seen.

Resources

For grief support, visit Compassionate Friends, at https://www.compassionatefriends.org, and Open to Hope, at https://www.opentohope.com.

13

COMPOSING A MARRIAGE

I would like nothing better than to wrap up this marriage story with a neat little bow for you. But that is exactly what cannot be done without risking a false narrative or feeding into the unhelpful romanticized myth of happily ever after. There are many loose ends and more to be revealed, unraveled, and rewoven. Composing a marriage is a constant act of creation—a weaving, a dance, an evolving art form, constantly adjusting and adapting to the flow of life, to the unknown.

In our 40 years together, Matt and I have had at least four different marriages. They were all good, none was perfect, and each was quite distinct as we have grown together and apart. Our early marriage, composed of graduate student life and new babies, gave way to a professional family, with school children and community involvement. At a critical juncture, the "affair" allowed us to explore a new relationship, which was eventually folded back into a whole new marriage. Following that creative impulse, we took a sabbatical year, which eased our seemingly unresolvable tension around midlife changes as we each restructured our work and creative lives. The gentle turns in our path and then the traumatic heartbreak of losing our son led us to relocate to a new home on the coast, where we are now exploring grandparenthood, generativity, and a rich creative chapter. I don't know where it will go from here.

On our journey, we have encountered several difficult periods that are highlighted in these pages. We faced conflict early in our marriage, as we took up our lives together with a new baby and each developed our professional identities. We drifted apart as we each became consumed with our own responsibilities and had little time for each other. We struggled to find a way forward in midlife when our goals and desires seemed so incompatible. We suffered the loss of our youngest son and rebuilt our lives and our marriage. Navigating these different marriages within the marriage calls us to expand, to revise, perhaps to explode the old mold.

We have adapted to and crafted change in our joint lives, and our marriage has adjusted. The amount of time together and devoted to independent activities has changed. The balance of financial responsibility has also changed. The content of our arguments and the way we argue have shifted, perhaps even grown. We have given each other space for different movement along a common path. We have each tried to become truer to ourselves while also encouraging the other to fuller understandings of our life lived in marriage.

Even though we do not know the path, there are markers along the way—a kind of map that could alert us to obstacles or difficult terrain ahead. The problem is that the map is an aerial view, only visible with an elevated perspective.

Matt and I recently had the opportunity to kayak the Elkhorn Slough, an estuary off the Pacific Ocean in Monterey Bay. We dropped into the slough upstream and paddled along what seemed a main stream that would lead us into the primary slough. We noticed many channels and tributaries on either side and meandered into some of these smaller streams, not knowing whether they would lead us back out or to a dead end. Although there is a detailed aerial map of the slough and its tributaries, it was not visible to us in the moment, from the water's surface. Only with a higher view would we be able to get our bearings. As with marriage, we traveled along, finding our way. Only in retrospect are we able to understand where we have been or what we have been through.

Many experts have attempted to map the marriage journey through various stages, and the models share similar elements. They all begin with romance or bonding and move into disillusionment or differentiation. From there, the models vary along a theme of conflict and reconciliation. I have adapted the following model from Ellyn Bader and Peter Pearson's, which they shared in their book *In Quest of the Mythical Mate.*

Merging

We begin in love, merged with the other. This stage is often referred to as the honeymoon period. In this early phase of infatuation, the other seems ideal. We can't see—and don't want to see—their flaws. We project all of our glimmering hopes and dreams onto our new love, so that we cannot see the actual person at all. We are literally blinded by romance. During this early enchantment, we are swept up in the emotions and hormones of romantic love. We become intoxicated with one another, spending hours on end basking in each other's presence. The couple creates a bubble around themselves, impermeable to outside influence or criticism.

When Matt and I first became romantically involved, working together on the college course, we kept our relationship a secret. This made our bubble even tighter. When I returned from law school for Christmas the next year, we wrapped ourselves again in one another and wove our dreams of making a life together. Absence makes the heart grow fonder because the real-life person is out of the way; they cannot disturb the idealized dream image we hold of them.

In this stage, the couple is bonding, building intimacy and commitment, and drawing boundaries between themselves and others. Most formal marriage education is focused on couples at this stage and falls mostly on deaf ears. This is not the time to try to question the relationship or to teach realities of marriage. They are not listening and not able to hear it.

Depending on the timing, the couple may still be in this symbiotic romantic phase when they marry. With longer courtship and living together, the couple may have tasted disillusionment even before the wedding.

Disillusionment

As we get to know our partner and step back enough to actually see them, the warts come into view. Our beloved comes down off the pedestal. Suddenly, we see them in all of their human imperfections, annoying habits, bodily functions, and idiosyncrasies. Each partner emerges from the blind romance and struggles with the reality of their partner's unfamiliar ways.

I wasn't prepared for the reality of this shift in our early marriage. What had seemed complete compatibility turned to constant tension as we each sought to develop our separate identities and also recognized the other's flaws and shortcomings.

In this stage, the couple is learning to manage their differences, developing critical skills for communication and conflict resolution. This is a normal stage early in a relationship. The couple's differences, which might have initially seemed interesting or spicy, now are irritating and confusing. If you are feeling disillusioned within your marriage, find ways to communicate about your feelings, to navigate conflicts, and to overlook some annoyances. Keep your reactivity down and dedicate time for intentional conversation and connection. Notice that the task is to manage your differences, not to resolve them.

Drift

In this next stage, the partners move away from each other and cultivate separate interests. Taking the focus off the relationship reduces the level of conflict but also creates distance.

When our focus became too much on the separate worlds of our respective work, Matt and I became disengaged as a couple. Our lives became more disconnected with less time for each other, and we quietly drifted apart.

If you find yourself drifting, try to balance your personal autonomy with your connection in the relationship. Be aware of the risk of quiet disconnection. Step up your engagement and attention to each other. Create rituals for engagement, such as a classic date night, a favorite shared activity, a regular hike, or a bowling night. Make time together your priority, your glass ball.

Return and renewal

Eventually, the partners turn back toward each other and learn to balance their independence with the intimacy of togetherness.

Matt and I were able to find our way back to each other through intentional conversation about our relationship. We also cultivated the support of a community of couples, and we committed to working to improve and enrich our marriage. We developed the dance of balancing our individual work and identities with our family life and togetherness.

In this stage, you need to balance *me* and *we*. Cultivate your own interests and show an interest in your partner's work and activities outside the marriage. Attend their class or show up for their lunch break. Become a familiar and supportive presence.

Mutual interdependence

Couples who successfully navigate the previous stages develop skills along the way to manage the successive challenges that life will present. Eventually, a couple may reach the final stage of mutual interdependence, in which the perfect is reconciled with the real. The early disillusionment grows into pride and contentment for a partnership crafted over years, along a path of unique blessings and challenges.

AN ADAPTED DEVELOPMENTAL MODEL OF MARRIAGE

Merger: "We are One"
Task: Bonding

Disillusionment: "Off the Pedestal"
Task: Managing differences

Drift or conflict: "You do your thing; I'll do mine"
Task: Self-discovery, external directed

Return: "Balance me and we"
Task: Balancing intimacy and independence

Mutual interdependence: Double vision
Task: Balancing the perfect and the real

Based on Bader and Pearson's *In Quest of the Mythical Mate* (1988).

We may move through the stages sequentially but may also fall back or race ahead, progressing and regressing along the way. We also cycle back through the stages many times as we continue to evolve our relationship. We might go through all the stages in a single day. Partners do not necessarily move through the stages at the same time or the same pace, which creates crisis points in the relationship. The potential for the couple or one partner to get stuck in a particular phase can also threaten the relationship.

Bader and Pearson tell us that "each stage is more complex and requires new skills based on integration and transformation of what existed before into a new form." Like a snake molting, the couple needs to shed their current skin in order to grow into the next. It may take a crisis to move forward to some new shape, and this is how the couple creates the next chapter of their marriage together.

Our marriage unfolded without the benefit of understanding this larger trajectory and the critical shifts along the way. Our anniversary year-in-review serendipitously provided some perspective for us looking back year by year and taking stock. Now, with a 40-year arc of time, the picture comes into clearer focus. It may be that, when we are in the middle of living these tasks and transitions, we are unable to take the long view. The benefit of counseling, coaching, or other less formal supports for marriage is being able to gain perspective and encouragement during the difficult times, in real time.

We live each moment on the surface, feeling our way without the benefit of that larger view, married to and navigating the unknown together. Perhaps we can't really get lost, although we might wander around or take a few detours and turnarounds as we make our way down the river. That is all part of the journey.

Marriage is not an event. It is a journey. It can be a creative adventure. The wedding is an event, one of the best days of our life, and the marriage unfolds from there. A young woman on her wedding day exclaimed, "Oh, Mother! I am at the end of all my troubles." The mother wisely answered, "Yes, but which end?"

The journey begins at the wedding or often before it. The relationship unfolds in many of the ways we have explored. Marriage is far from static. It is a dynamic, creative, collaborative endeavor undertaken together. Couples might expect that stepping across the threshold ushers in a magical transformation or requires that they suddenly change their roles or relationship. I have seen marriages dissolve within months of the wedding day, clearly not what the happy couple expected. Even more puzzling is when couples who have been together for years, often living together, separate shortly after getting married. One couple I know had been together for eight years and then separated within two months of being married. The young wife believed that with marriage her boyfriend would change, give up his bachelor ways of partying, and get serious about working and providing financially. When he continued his same behaviors, she wanted out.

Remember, the marriage is not going where you alone think it will go. The process will invite both partners, and others that enter into their circle, into a dance of circumstance, navigating life's currents to live their best lives.

Composing a marriage is a worthy life's work. It is a symphony of discordant elements, creative, experimental, and experiential. In the alchemical process of marriage, each person is transformed through the constant interface with the other, the chosen partner and antagonist, the grain of sand in our oyster shell, with and through whom we craft the dance of our lives.

The dance of marriage is happening on several levels all at the same time. There is the outer or mundane worldly activity. This is the logistical, practical level of daily life, from household chores to finances, work and recreation, friends and family, parenting, providing, partnering in so many practical ways. On a deeper level, we are engaged in an inner psychological and emotional level of intimacy. Here, our beliefs, memories, and wounds that create our inner lens on the world meet our spouse's and spark reactions, reflections, and perhaps new perspectives on ourselves. We play out our own psychological issues with our intimate partner, who may uniquely trigger our shadow self. Finally, there is what I would call a sacred aspect, a transcendent, elevated encounter with one another at a soul level, where we touch the promise of true marriage. We spend most of our days in the mundane, with perhaps intentional or spontaneous ventures into the psychological, and occasional flights to the sacred. All three levels are happening all the time, each contributing to the dance, evolving our hearts and souls toward greater wholeness for both partners.

Glimpses into the sacred marriage are truly awesome. We may see it in our child's or grandchild's face mirroring our partner's familiar features. Or we may see it when we recognize our spouse as the young lover of decades ago and in the same moment the aging physical form holding that same essence. Or we may see it by simply reflecting with gratitude on the many memories we have shared and the deep companionship of age.

This may sound romanticized, but it's really not. Even as Matt and I enjoy each other's company with the benefit of years together, we still get on each other's nerves. When I am cleaning up after a negligent habit of Matt's—cabinet doors flung open or dirty clothes discarded right next to the laundry basket—I try to remember that these are the annoyances I will someday find endearing. But, for now, they are just annoying, and I have my annoying habits as well. We each press our agendas, directions, and points of view while accusing the other of being controlling in resisting our better wisdom. Sometimes, my appreciation of Matt's many wonderful qualities dims in the shadow of the grinding exasperation of long-standing pet peeves. Then we sit on the deck, watch the sunset, and reflect on our many blessings, counting our marriage among them. It's not magic; it's real.

It is my hope that knowing we are all muddling through, doing the best we can and having moments of brilliance, managing the depths and touching the promise, offers you encouragement and consolation in composing your marriage. Perhaps, over time or at moments, we may recognize that with our eyes wide open to the imperfections of ourselves, our partner, and our marriage, we have arrived at the original promise of happily ever after. We are content with our choice; we have lived that choice to its fullest potential.

Composing a marriage is a constant act of creation, a weaving, a dance, an evolving art form, constantly adjusting and adapting to the flow of life, to the unknown.

Reflection

Coming to the end of this book, take some time to reflect back on your marriage over time. Take in the big picture. What might the map of your marriage look like with the arc of time?

- How has our marriage changed over time? What caused the change?
- What are the key elements of our marriage? Commitment? Shared purpose? Romance? Parenting? Partnership? Intimacy? Companionship?
- Is there an image that symbolizes our marriage for me?

WIND

Judith Hanson Lasater

Winter is my favorite season to walk on the beach.
The silver-green sea and the billowing threatening gray sky seem to merge in the distance, creating an infinite horizon as I gaze seaward.
The stark cold beach is empty and lonely, but my heart is full and warm when I think of you.
Now turning my gaze, I see a large copse of cedar trees standing guard courageously by the water, a first line of sentinels, as ocean gives way to land.
The cedars are closely set and well established, and clearly have seen many other winters.
Years of the unremitting ocean's wind have shaped and entangled them like a corps of hoary unmoving dancers, arching landward in an eternal arabesque.

Perhaps gathered together for companionship and comfort, their sturdy trunks are permanently curved, leaning away from the ocean.
This very shape shows their age.
Graceful and unafraid, they accept their bent shape with resonant patience.
Yet their roughened trunks cannot but express their senescence.
Nicks and cuts and occasional empty spaces are plainly visible where branches once grew.
Here and there, lovers have carved their initials into the bark of some trees.
These ancient cedars are no longer pristine.
You and I share kinship with those trees.
Like those cedars, you and I have been shaped by the constant wind of our years, and by the gradual wisdom only time brings.
Like those cedars, we remember those who once carved their initials in our hearts, leaving evidence of their transitory presence in our lives, and then drifted away to other shores.
Through it all, we have grown slowly steadfast like those trees.
Side by side we stand, seemingly separate, yet with our branches deliciously intertwined, and living with a sense of deep contentedness for who we were, who we are, who we might yet become.
We thrive by the salty sea, and we fearlessly accept the ceaseless wind in our branches and the unmistakable evidence of our years.
How grateful I am to be living by the ocean, still and rooted and together with you.

Continue the conversation

www.marriage-unveiled.org

RECOMMENDED READING

Nonfiction

Bader, Ellyn and Pearson, Peter T., *In Quest of the Mythical Mate*, Brunner/Mazel (1988).

Berry, Wendell, "Poetry and Marriage," in *Standing by Words*, Counterpoint Press (1983).

Berry, Wendell, "The Body and the Earth," in *The Art of the Commonplace: The Agrarian Essays of Wendell Berry*, Counterpoint Press (2003).

Gilbert, Elizabeth, *Committed: A Love Story*, Bloomsbury (2010).

Gottman, John, *Why Marriages Succeed or Fail, and How You Can Make Yours Last*, Simon & Schuster (1994).

Heyn, Dalma, *The Erotic Silence of the American Wife*, Plume (1997).

Krasnow, Iris, *Surrendering to Marriage: Husbands, Wives and Other Imperfections*, Hyperion (2002).

Moore, Thomas, *Soul Mates: Honoring the Mysteries of Love and Relationship*, HarperCollins (1994).

Perel, Esther, *Mating in Captivity: Unlocking Erotic Intelligence*, HarperCollins (2006).

Tatkin, Stan, *We Do: Saying Yes to a Relationship of Depth, True Connection, and Enduring Love*, Sounds True (2018).

Waldman, Mark Robert, *The Art of Staying Together, Embracing Love, Intimacy and Spirit in Relationships*, Tarcher/Putnam Books (1998).

Wallace, Catherine M., *For Fidelity: How Intimacy and Commitment Enrich Our Lives*, Vintage (1998).

Wallerstein, Judith, and Blakeslee, Sandra, *The Good Marriage: How and Why Love Lasts*, Warner Books (1996).

Fiction

Jones, Tayari, *An American Marriage*, Algonquin Books (2019).

Stegner, Wallace, *Crossing to Safety*, Random House (1987).

Tyler, Anne, *Breathing Lessons*, Berkeley Books (1988).

Online Resources

Marriage and relationship advice: https://www.marriage.com

The Gottman Institute, supporting healthy relationships: https://www.gottman.com/blog/

Catholic marriage and family support: https://www.foryourmarriage.org

National Center on African American Marriages and Parenting:
https://www.hamptonu.edu/ncaamp/

CenterLink, The Community of LGBTQ Centers:
https://www.lgbtcenters.org

ACKNOWLEDGMENTS

Like a marriage, writing a book is a journey, and not a solo expedition at that. It is an unfolding path pulling in many voices along the way. Some companions have walked a long distance with me, some have crossed my path for a short while. But each has left their own unique footprints on the story.

Family and friends were early readers and constant encouragers. Matt of course wrote the story with me over these 40 plus years. He also lovingly read and reread each word, suggesting nuance and depth to clarify my meaning. My sister, Colleen Hensley, and brother-in-law, Bill Hensley, were front-line consultants and proponents of the book with insight, enthusiasm, and almost prophetic advice. My grown children, Tyler and Cassedy, cheered me on with perspectives from their own marriage experiences. The Madison/McBride clan (Mary McBride and Mike Madison, Erin Madison, David Madison, and Ron Madison) offered whole-hearted encouragement across three generations of marriages. My "Sisters in Law" (Mauna Berkov, Diana Richmond, Lee Jordan, Pam Pierson, Dee Samuels, and Peggy Bennington), all divorce attorneys and creatives in their own right, gave invaluable support. My dear friends Eileen and John Donahoe, Bhavani Maki, Lorri Jean, Myra Stroeber, Faith Freed, Dodie Mazzuca, Sally Lillis, and Satya Graha provided essential encouragement when I most needed it.

The journey took several more turns when my wise friend Jim Moroney suggested I find a "really good editor." I found in fact four really good editors in Tom Shroder, Holly Payne, Tania Casselle, and Jill Mellick, each arriving at just the right time to provide critical advice and perspective. I finally landed with the skilled Greenleaf team who have polished and designed the final book to bring it across the finish line.

I am thankful to the teachers quoted within who have gone before me shining light on the path. I am thankful to my clients and students who have trusted me to guide them across thresholds. I am thankful to all of you fellow travelers as we each make our way imperfectly toward our more perfect union in this journey of the heart.

ABOUT THE AUTHOR

Sherry Cassedy has practiced family law and mediation for over 35 years in Palo Alto, California (marriage-unveiled.org). She teaches and offers spiritual retreats and guidance, drawing on her extensive background in both yoga and Catholicism to integrate wisdom teachings into daily experience and practice (thresholdguidance.com).

Sherry received her BA from Stanford University and her JD from Georgetown University Law Center. She also has an MA in transpersonal psychology with a certificate in spiritual guidance. Sherry is a licensed minister and works with couples in preparing and officiating marriage ceremonies.

Sherry lives in Santa Cruz, California, with her husband, Matt Sullivan. They enjoy the Pacific Coast and spending time with their adult children and their families, including three precious grandchildren.

Made in the USA
Las Vegas, NV
31 May 2022